Alphabet Review

Connect the Dots

■ Draw a line from a to z in alphabetical order while saying each letter out loud.

a	b	c	d	e	f	g	h	i	j	k	l	m	n	o	p	q	r	s	t	u	v	w	x	y	z

■ Draw a line from a to z in alphabetical order while saying each letter out loud.

a	b	c	d	e	f	g	h	i	j	k	l	m	n	o	p	q	r	s	t	u	v	w	x	y	z

Alphabet Review

Writing a–z

Name

Date / /

To parents/guardians: It is a good idea to have your child say each letter out loud as they complete the activity.

■ Trace the letters a to z.

a a

b b

c c

d d

e e

f f

g g

h h

i i

j j

k k

l l

m m

n n

o o

p p

q q

r r

s s

t t

u u

v v

w w

x x

y y

z z

a	b	c	d	e	f	g	h	i	j	k	l	m	n	o	p	q	r	s	t	u	v	w	x	y	z

■ Write the letters a to z.

a b c d

e f g h

i j k l

m n o p

q r s t

u v w x

y z

a	b	c	d	e	f	g	h	i	j	k	l	m	n	o	p	q	r	s	t	u	v	w	x	y	z

Consonant Sounds

The "b" Sound

Name　　　　　　　　Date
　　　　　　　　　　　/　　/

To parents/guardians: Throughout this book, it is important that you encourage your child to say each word out loud. This will help your child learn the relationships between letters and sounds.

■ Say the word represented by the picture out loud. Then circle the letter that makes the "b" sound at the beginning of the word.

b e e

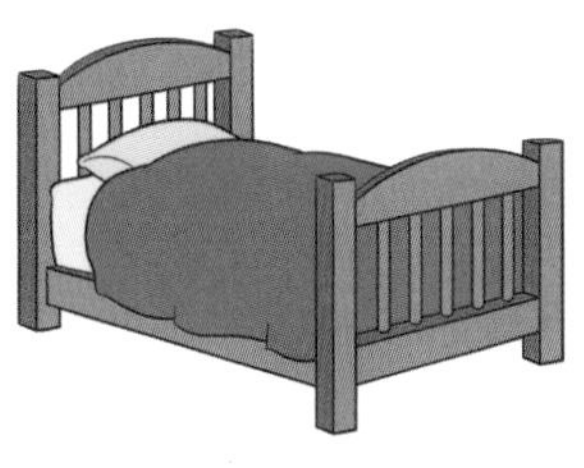

b e d

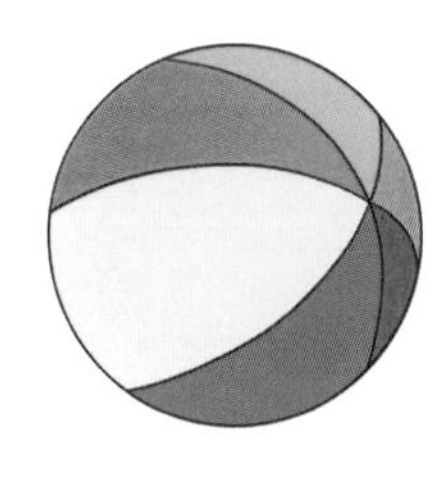

b a l l

b o o k

b a t

b u s

b i k e

b i r d

b o a t

a	b	c	d	e	f	g	h	i	j	k	l	m	n	o	p	q	r	s	t	u	v	w	x	y	z

To parents/guardians: On this page, your child will trace a path as they repeat words beginning with the "b" sound. If your child struggles to say a word, you can offer them help by saying something like, "What letter does this word start with? Can you make the 'b' sound?"

■ Draw a line along the path from the dot (●) to the star (★).
Each time you pass an image, say the word out loud.

a b c d e f g h i j k l m n o p q r s t u v w x y z

Consonant Sounds

The "k" Sound

Name Date / /

To parents/guardians: As each new letter is introduced it is important to make sure your child says each word out loud. This will help them connect the right sound to each letter.

■ Say the word represented by the picture out loud. Then circle the letter that makes the "k" sound at the beginning of the word.

key

kid

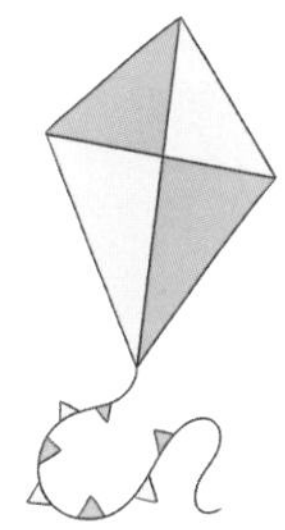

kite

kiss

kick

king

kitten

kitchen

koala

a b c d e f g h i j k l m n o p q r s t u v w x y z

■ Draw a line along the path from the dot (●) to the star (★).
Each time you pass an image, say the word out loud.

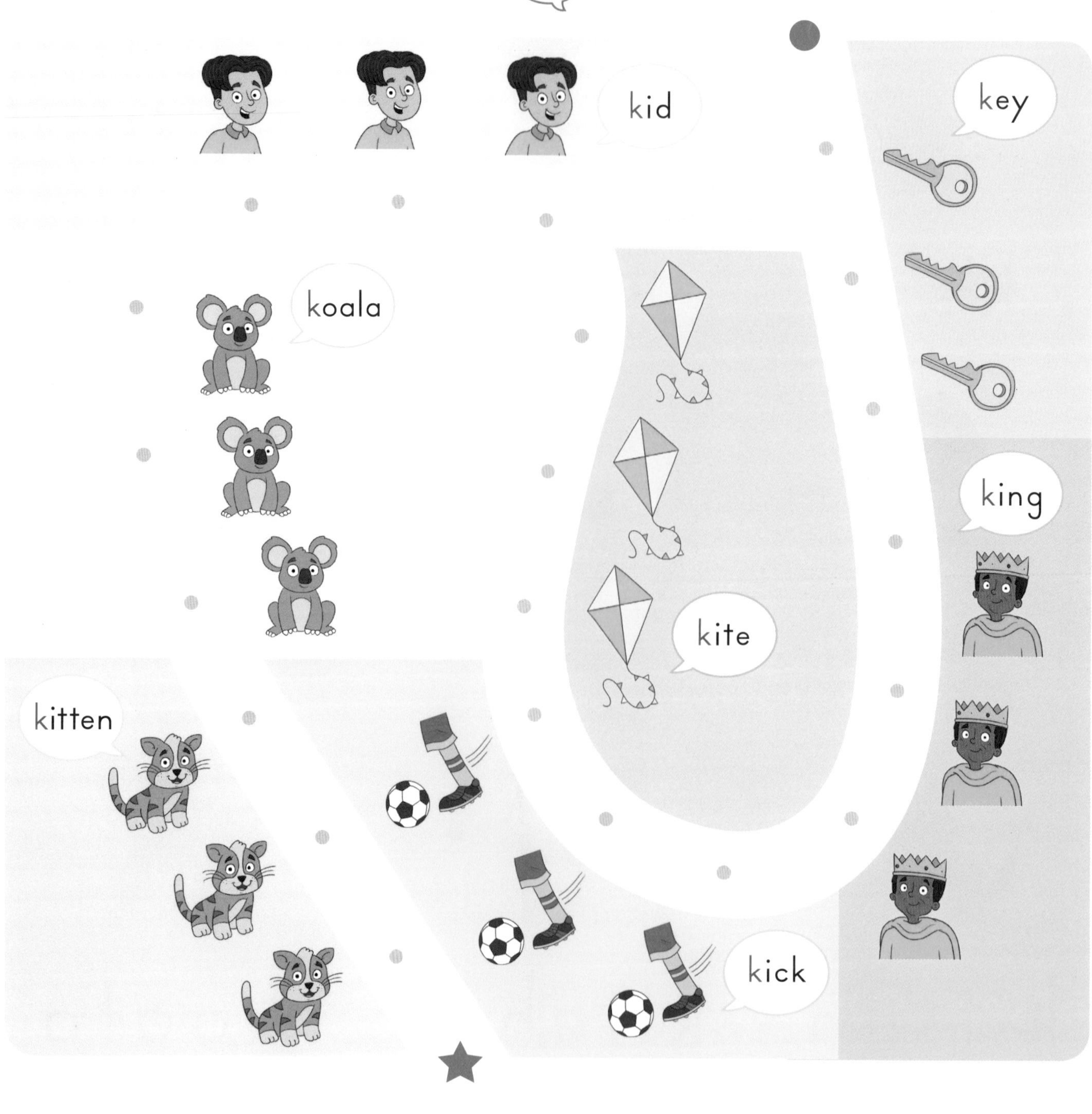

a	b	c	d	e	f	g	h	i	j	k	l	m	n	o	p	q	r	s	t	u	v	w	x	y	z

Consonant Sounds

The "p" Sound

Name　　　　Date　　/　　/

To parents/guardians: It is easy to confuse the "p" and "b" sounds. Listen carefully to be sure your child is saying "p."

■ Say the word represented by the picture out loud. Then circle the letter that makes the "p" sound at the beginning of the word.

pot 　　pencil 　　pink

penguin 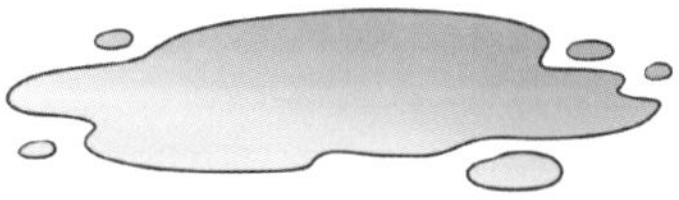　　puddle 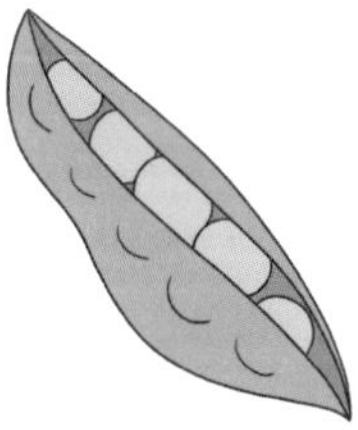　　peas

pond 　　push 　　plane

a b c d e f g h i j k l m n o p q r s t u v w x y z

- Draw a line along the path from the dot (●) to the star (★).
  Each time you pass an image, (say) the word out loud.

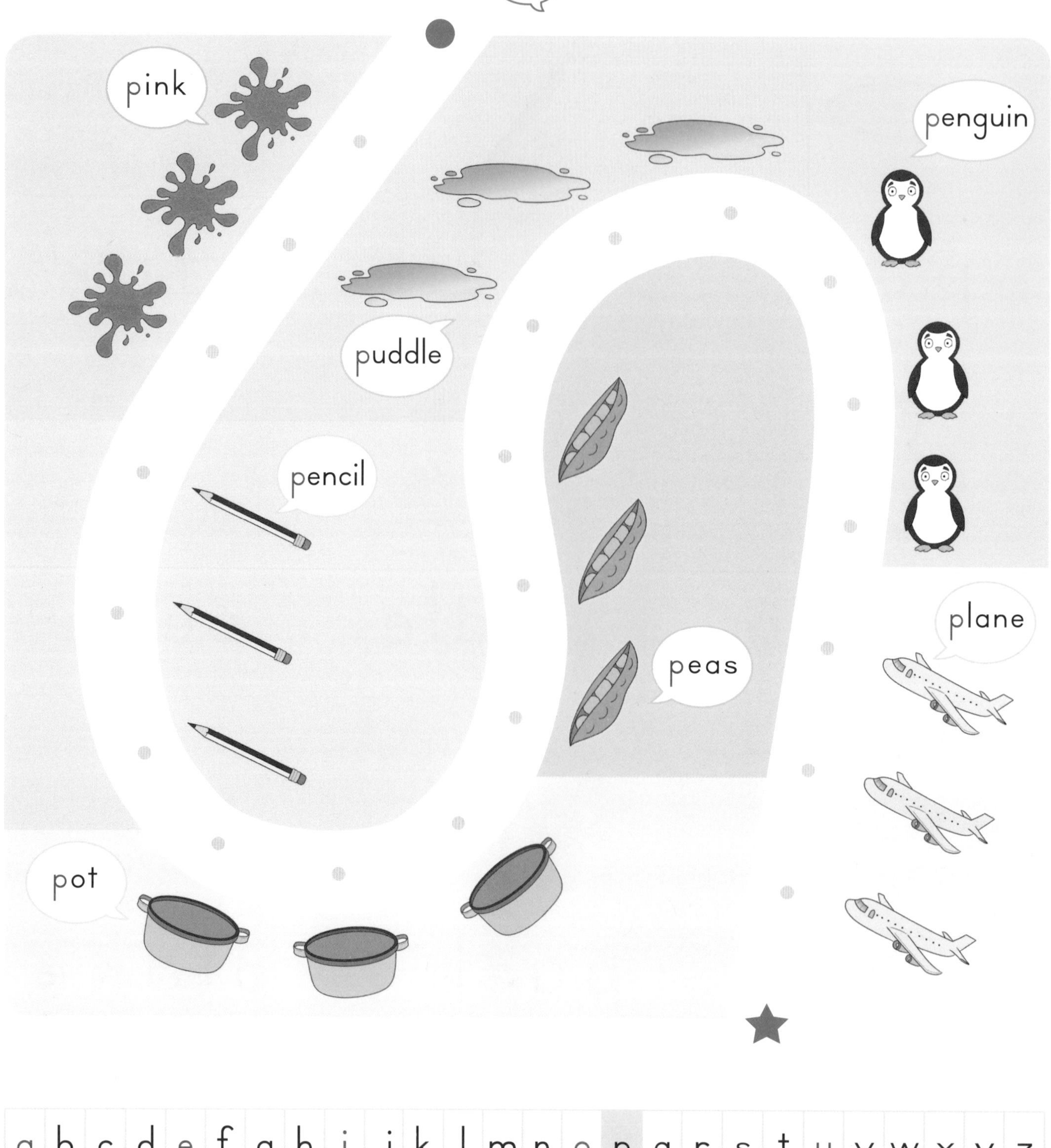

a b c d e f g h i j k l m n o p q r s t u v w x y z

Consonant Review

The "b", "k", and "p" Sounds

Name   Date
/   /

To parents/guardians: In this section, your child will review three letter sounds together. Make sure your child says each word out loud correctly to reinforce the letter sounds.

■ Say the word represented by the picture out loud. Then write in the missing letter.

b e e

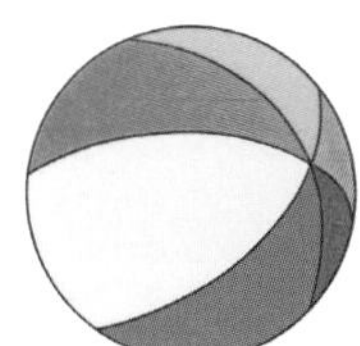

a l l

i k e

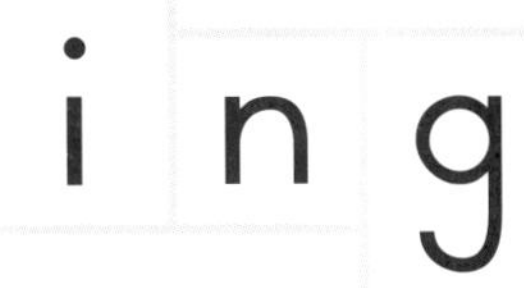

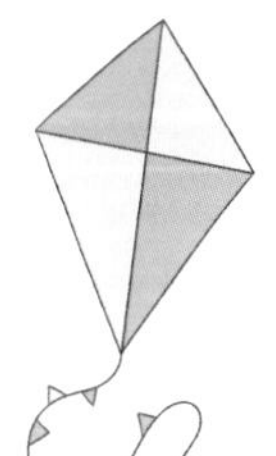

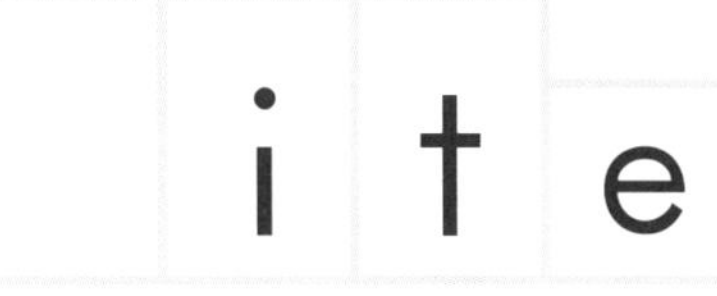

i n k

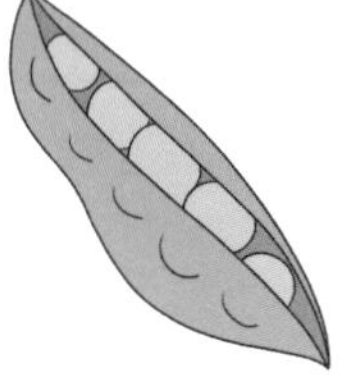

e a s

a b c d e f g h i j k l m n o p q r s t u v w x y z

- Trace each path from dot (●) to star (★) by following the words that begin with the same letter sound. (Say) each word as you go.

a	b	c	d	e	f	g	h	i	j	k	l	m	n	o	p	q	r	s	t	u	v	w	x	y	z

Consonant Sounds

The "t" Sound

Name

Date / /

To parents/guardians: As each new letter is introduced it is important to make sure your child says each word out loud. You can point out that the first word, *tent,* has the "t" sound at the beginning and end of the word.

■ Say the word represented by the picture out loud. Then circle the letter that makes the "t" sound at the beginning of the word.

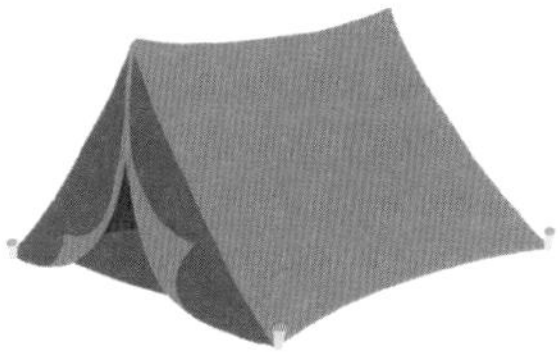

t e n t

t o p

t a l k

t i e

t a l l

t a b l e

t a i l

t o o t h

t i g e r

a b c d e f g h i j k l m n o p q r s t u v w x y z

■ Draw a line along the path from the dot (●) to the star (★).
Each time you pass an image, say the word out loud.

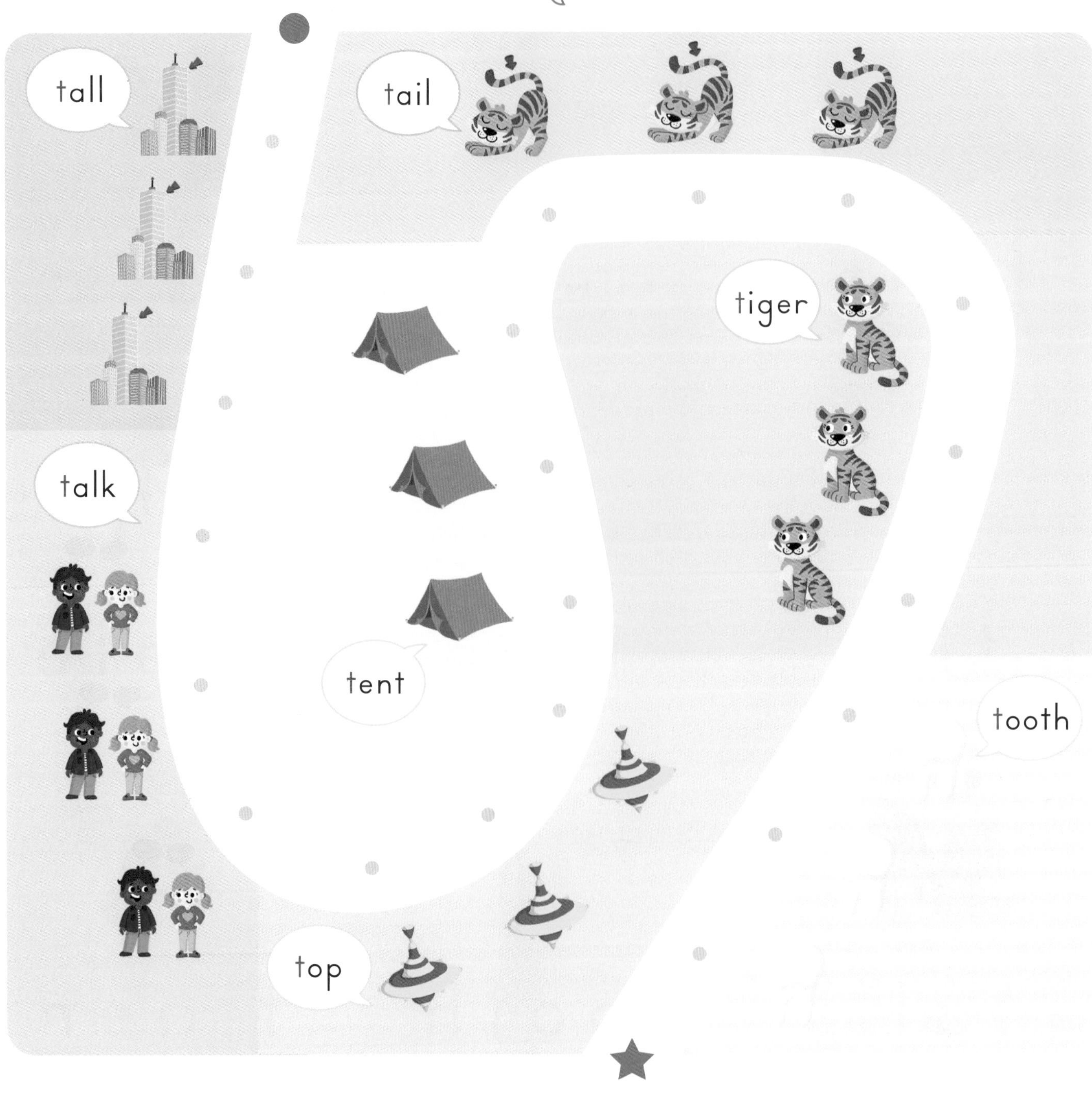

a b c d e f g h i j k l m n o p q r s t u v w x y z

8 Consonant Sounds

The "d" Sound

Name　　　　　　　　　Date
　　　　　　　　　　/　　/

To parents/guardians: The bottom row introduces your child to the common blend of the "d" and "r" sounds. Blends will be explored more deeply in the next level workbook. Help your child pronounce these words if they have trouble.

■ Say the word represented by the picture out loud. Then circle the letter that makes the "d" sound at the beginning of the word.

duck

desk

deer

day

doll

donut

dress

dry

drum

a b c d e f g h i j k l m n o p q r s t u v w x y z

■ Draw a line along the path from the dot (●) to the star (★).
Each time you pass an image, say the word out loud.

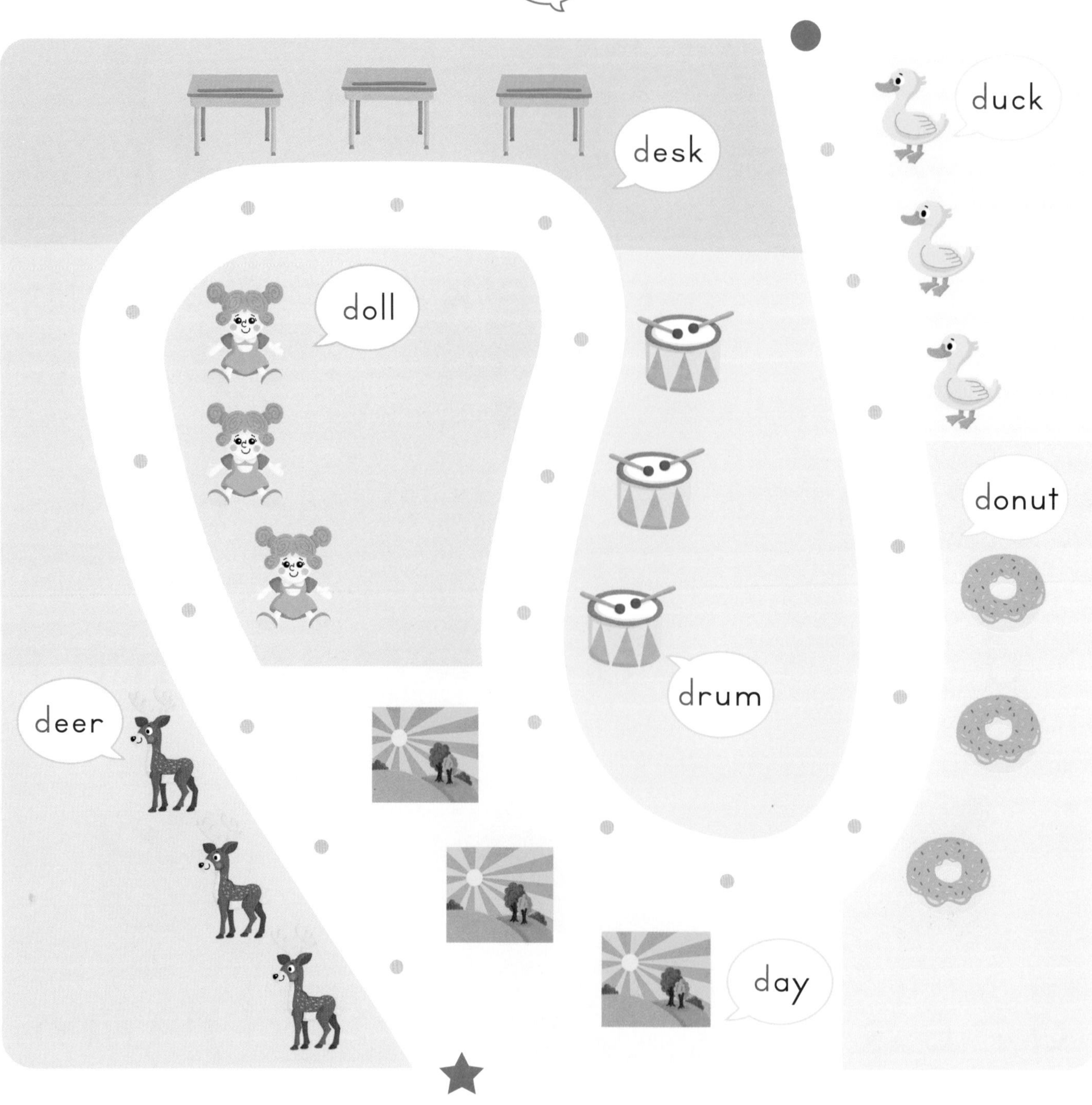

a b c d e f g h i j k l m n o p q r s t u v w x y z

Consonant Sounds

The Hard "g" Sound

Name Date / /

To parents/guardians: The letter *g* can make a hard "g" sound, as in "goat," and a soft "g" sound, as in "gem." This first workbook in the series focuses only on the hard "g" sound.

■ Say the word represented by the picture out loud. Then circle the letter that makes the hard "g" sound at the beginning of the word.

girl  gold  gift

goat  go  glue

gap  grow 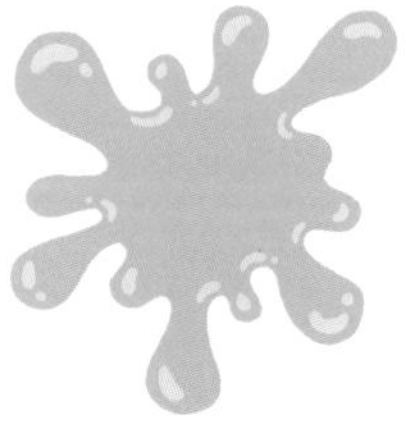 green

a b c d e f g h i j k l m n o p q r s t u v w x y z

■ Draw a line along the path from the dot (●) to the star (★).
Each time you pass an image, say the word out loud.

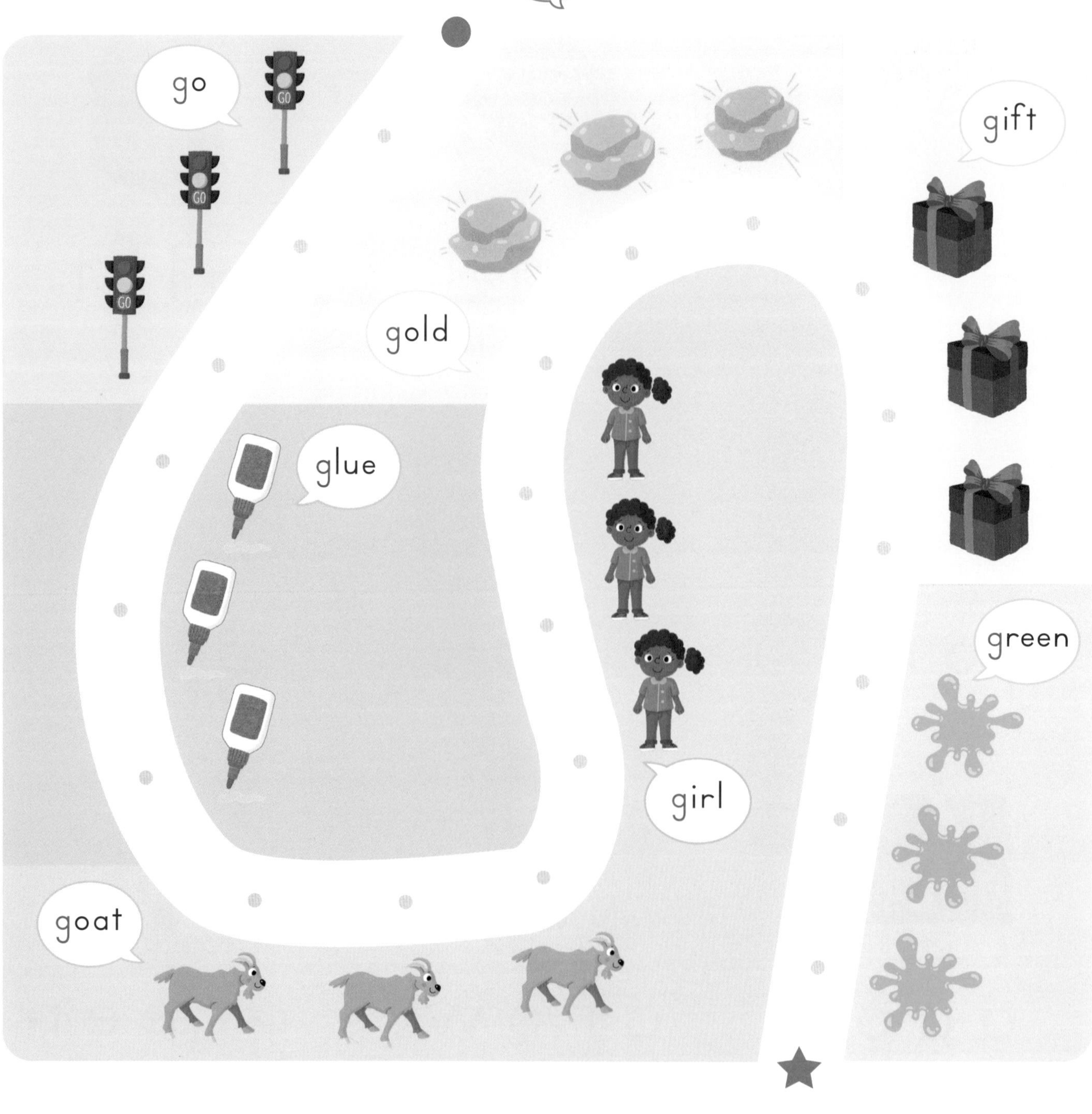

a b c d e f g h i j k l m n o p q r s t u v w x y z

10 Consonant Review

The "t", "d", and "g" Sounds

Name

Date

/ /

To parents/guardians: In this section, your child will review three letter sounds together. Make sure your child says each word out loud correctly to reinforce the letter sounds.

■ Say the word represented by the picture out loud. Then write in the missing letter.

t i e

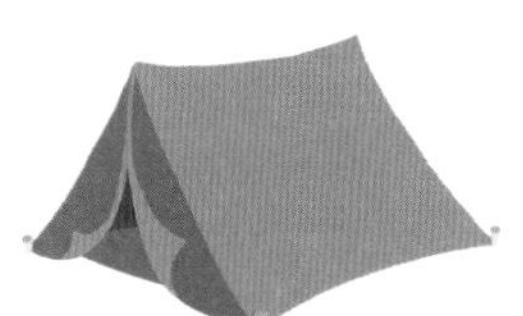

e n t

i g e r

d u c k

r u m

o l l

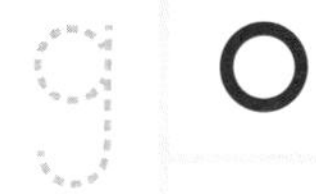

g o

i f t

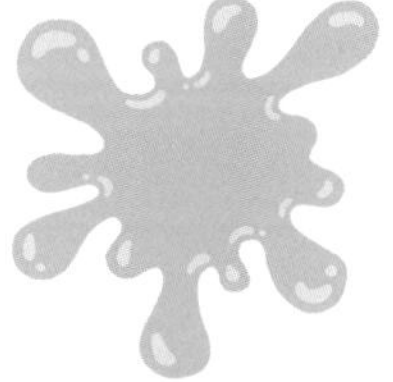

r e e n

a b c d e f g h i j k l m n o p q r s t u v w x y z

■ Trace each path from dot (●) to star (★) by following the words that begin with the same letter sound. Say each word as you go.

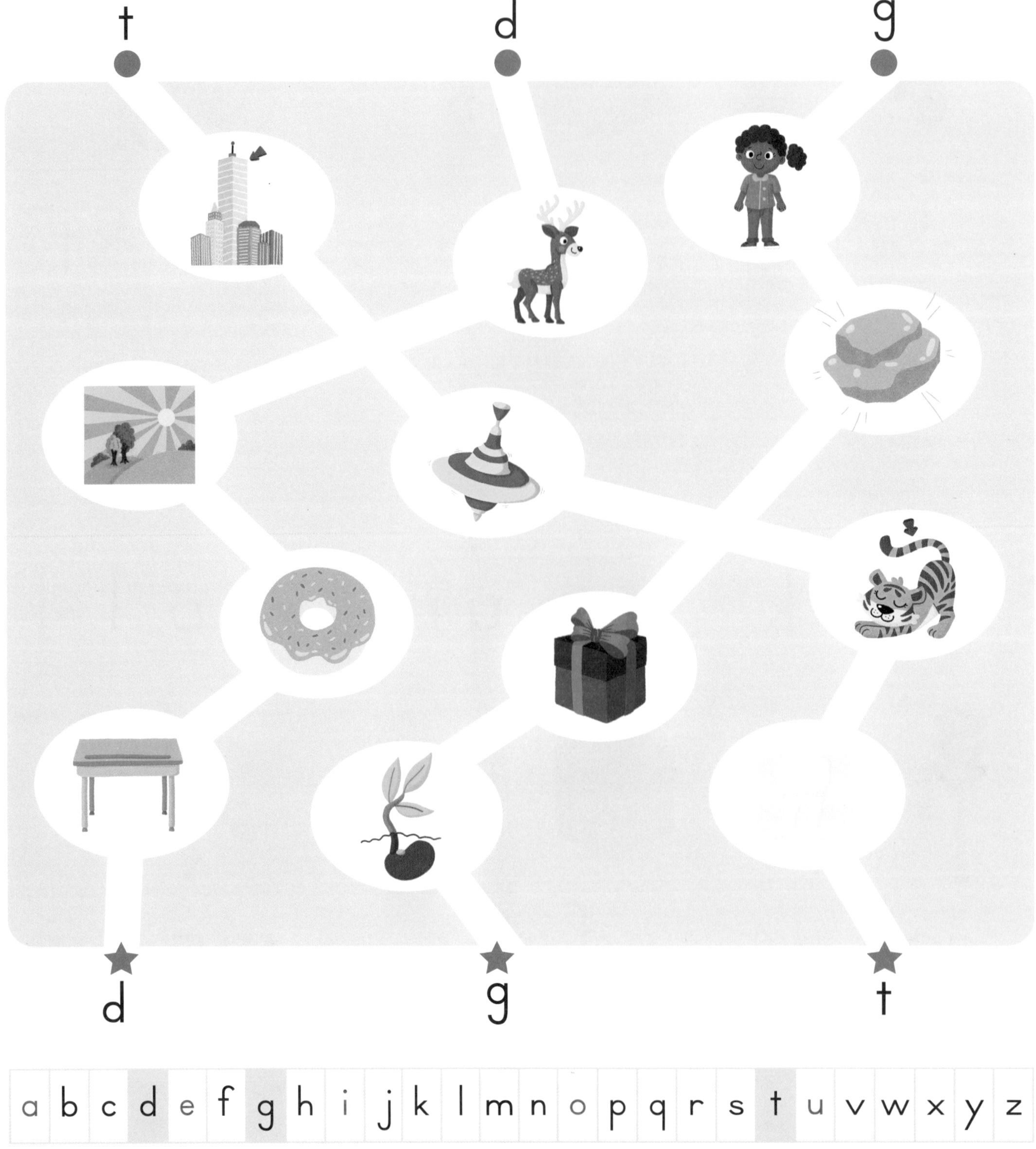

Consonant Sounds

The Hard "c" Sound

Name

Date / /

To parents/guardians: The letter c can make a hard "c" sound, as in "card," and a soft "c" sound, as in the initial sound in "circle." This first workbook in the series focuses only on the hard "c" sound. It is the same as the "k" sound which appears later in this book.

■ Say the word represented by the picture out loud. Then circle the letter that makes the hard "c" sound at the beginning of the word.

car

call

coat

card

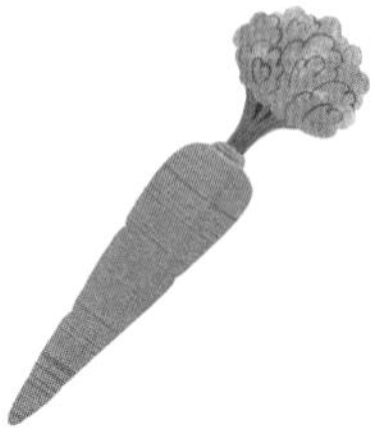

carrot

crab

cold

cake

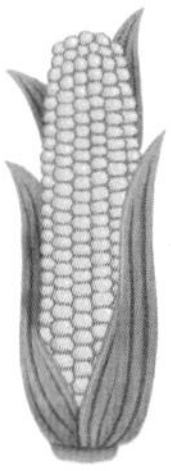

corn

a b c d e f g h i j k l m n o p q r s t u v w x y z

- Draw a line along the path from the dot (●) to the star (★). Each time you pass an image, say the word out loud.

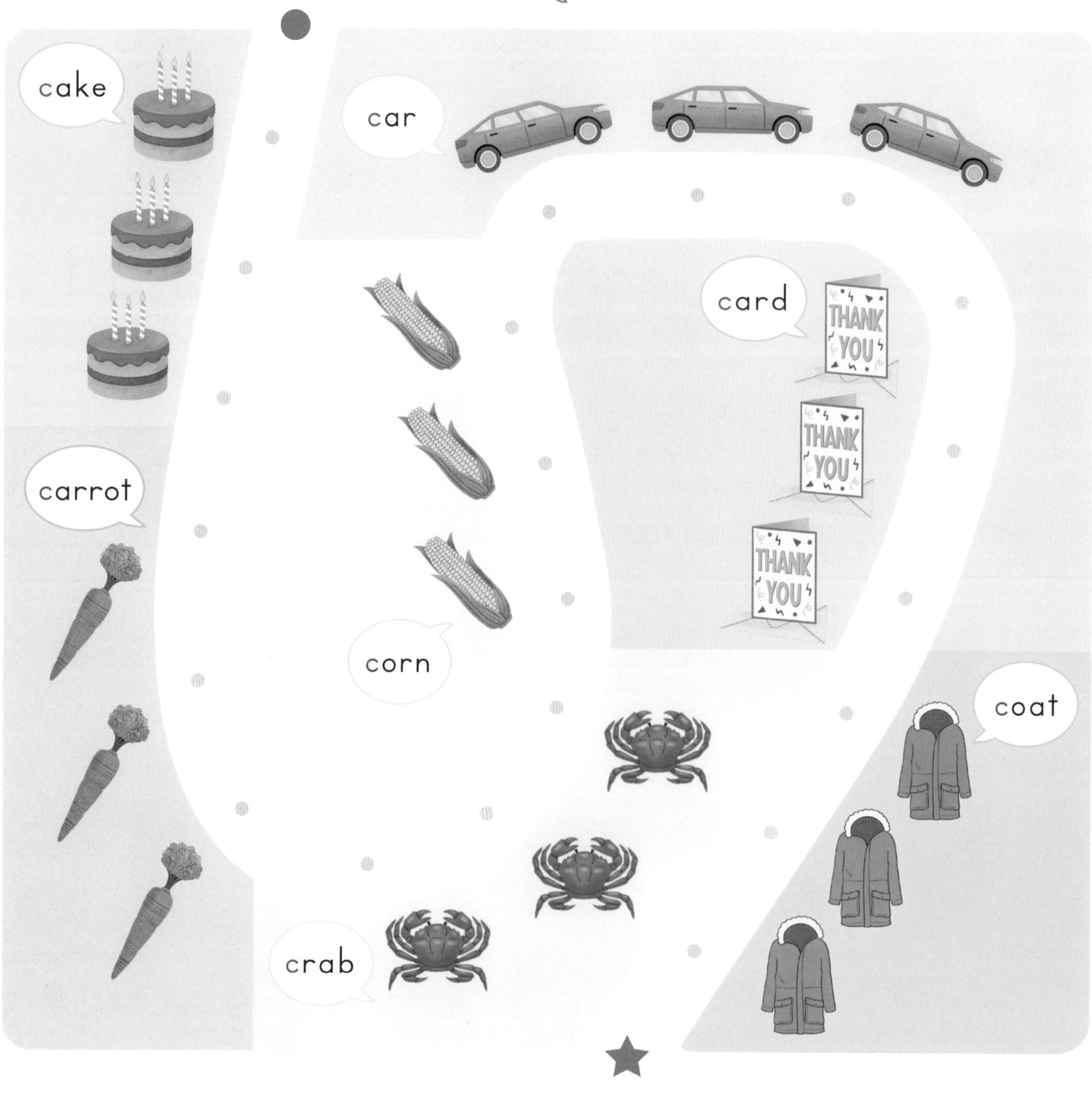

a b c d e f g h i j k l m n o p q r s t u v w x y z

Consonant Sounds

The "j" Sound

Name Date / /

To parents/guardians: If your child struggles to pronounce the "j" sound, please offer them guidance on how to say it correctly and encourage frequent practice. Let them see how you form the sound with your mouth.

■ Say the word represented by the picture out loud. Then circle the letter that makes the "j" sound at the beginning of the word.

jar

jump

jaw

juice

jam

jet

jog

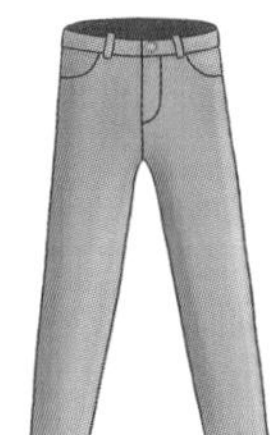

jeans

jewel

a	b	c	d	e	f	g	h	i	j	k	l	m	n	o	p	q	r	s	t	u	v	w	x	y	z

■ Draw a line along the path from the dot (●) to the star (★).
Each time you pass an image, say the word out loud.

a b c d e f g h i j k l m n o p q r s t u v w x y z

13 Consonant Sounds

The "m" Sound

Name Date / /

To parents/guardians: For extra practice, encourage your child to think of other words that begin with the "m" sound.

■ Say the word represented by the picture out loud. Then circle the letter that makes the "m" sound at the beginning of the word.

mail

mouse

man

mask

muffin

milk

moon

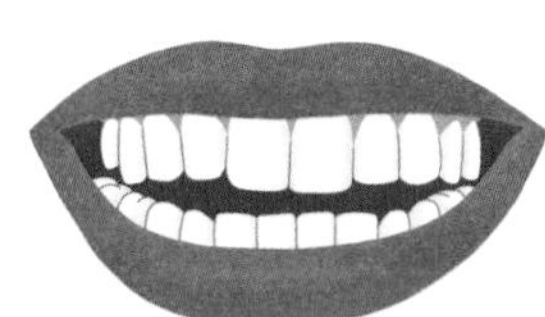

mouth

money

a b c d e f g h i j k l m n o p q r s t u v w x y z

■ Draw a line along the path from the dot (●) to the star (★).
Each time you pass an image, say the word out loud.

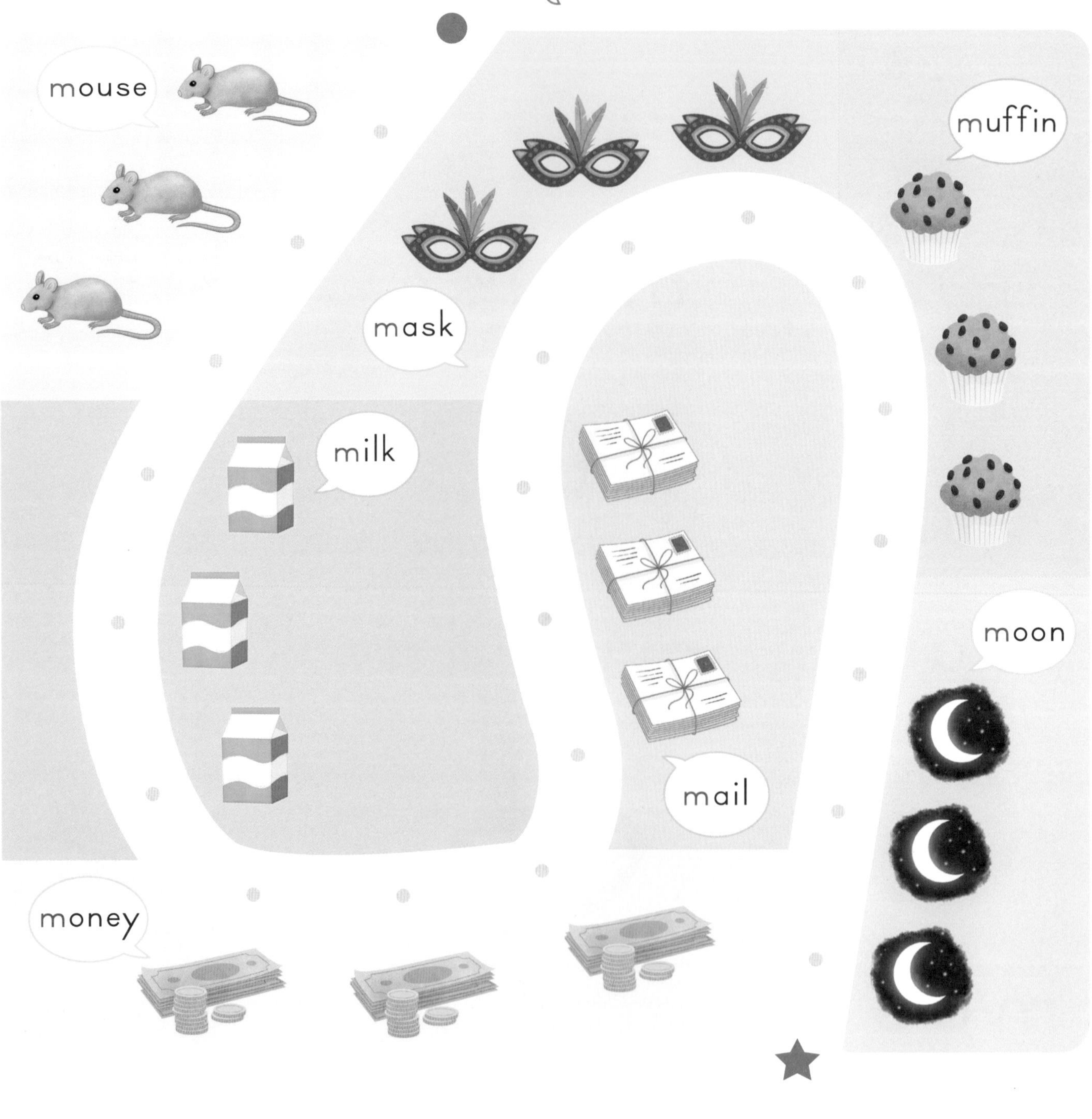

a b c d e f g h i j k l m n o p q r s t u v w x y z

Consonant Review

The Hard "c", "j", and "m" Sounds

Name Date / /

To parents/guardians: In this section, your child will review three letter sounds together. Make sure your child says each word out loud correctly to reinforce the letter sounds.

■ Say the word represented by the picture out loud. Then write in the missing letter.

c a r

a k e

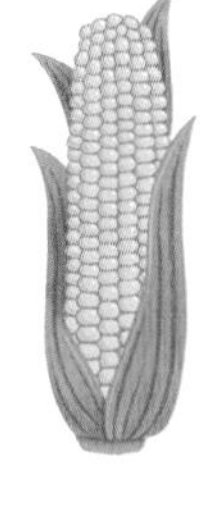

o r n

j a r

a m

e w e l

m a i l

i l k

o o n

a b c d e f g h i j k l m n o p q r s t u v w x y z

■ Trace each path from dot (●) to star (★) by following the words that begin with the same letter sound. (Say) each word as you go.

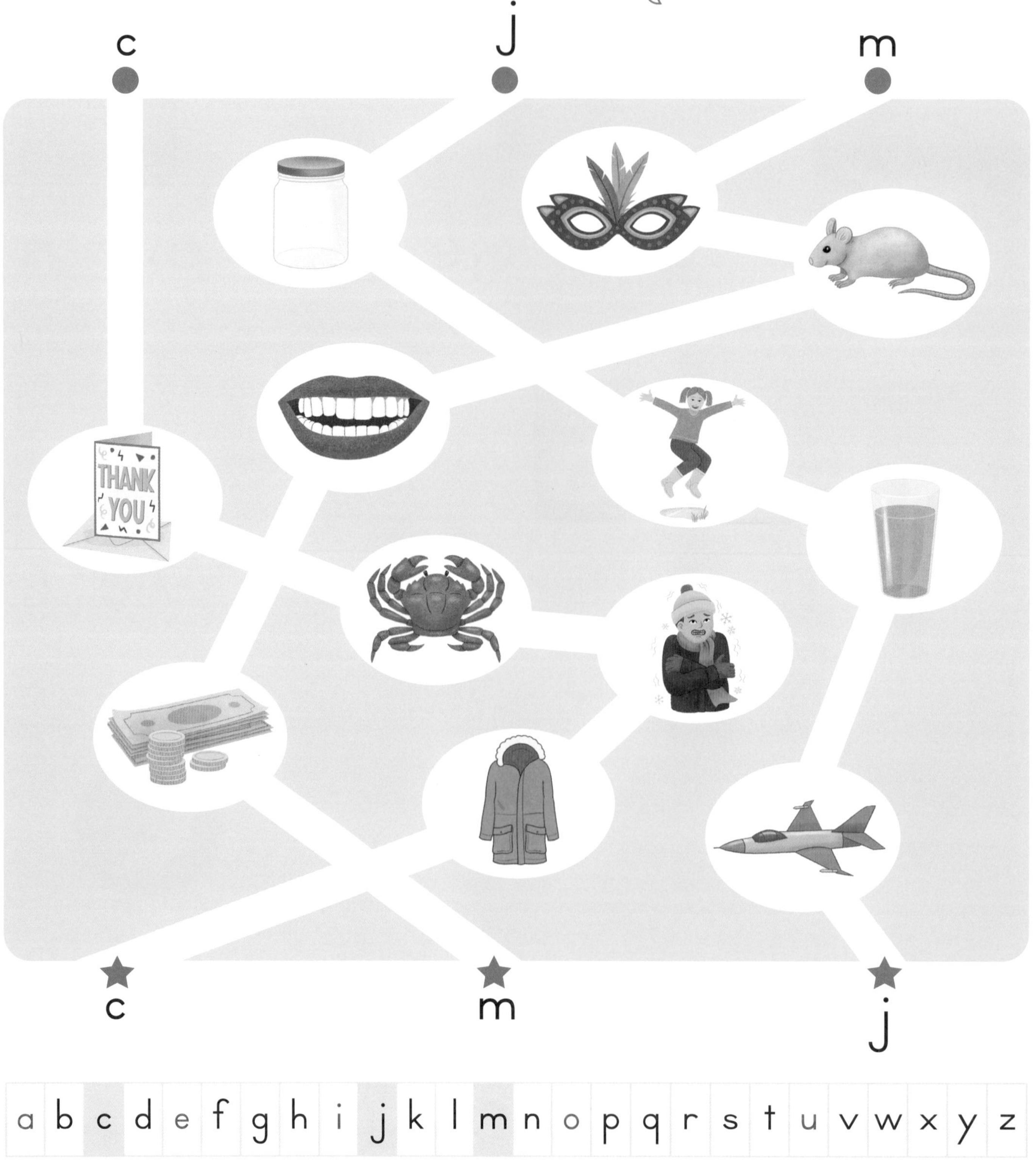

a	b	c	d	e	f	g	h	i	j	k	l	m	n	o	p	q	r	s	t	u	v	w	x	y	z

Consonant Sounds

The “s” Sound

Name Date / /

To parents/guardians: This section includes words in which the *s* sounds like a hissing snake. The letter *s* can also make a sound like a *z*.

■ Say the word represented by the picture out loud. Then circle the letter that makes the “s” sound at the beginning of the word.

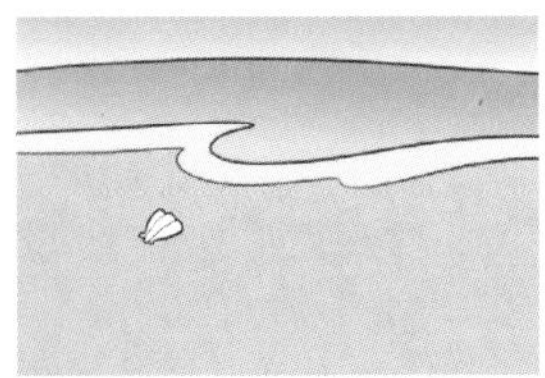

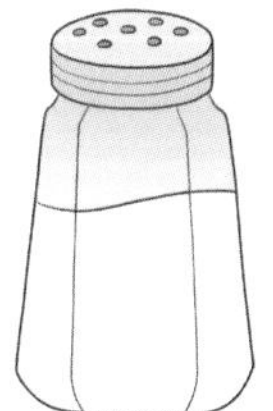

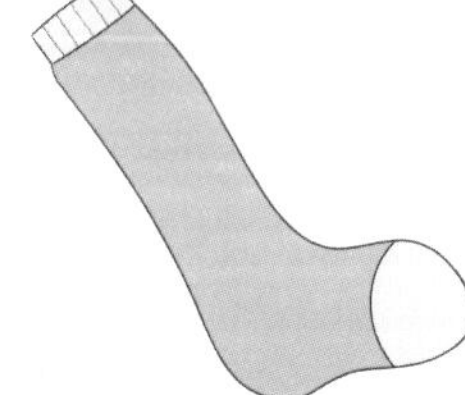

salt sock snake

sing spin soap

a b c d e f g h i j k l m n o p q r s t u v w x y z

■ Draw a line along the path from the dot (●) to the star (★).
Each time you pass an image, say the word out loud.

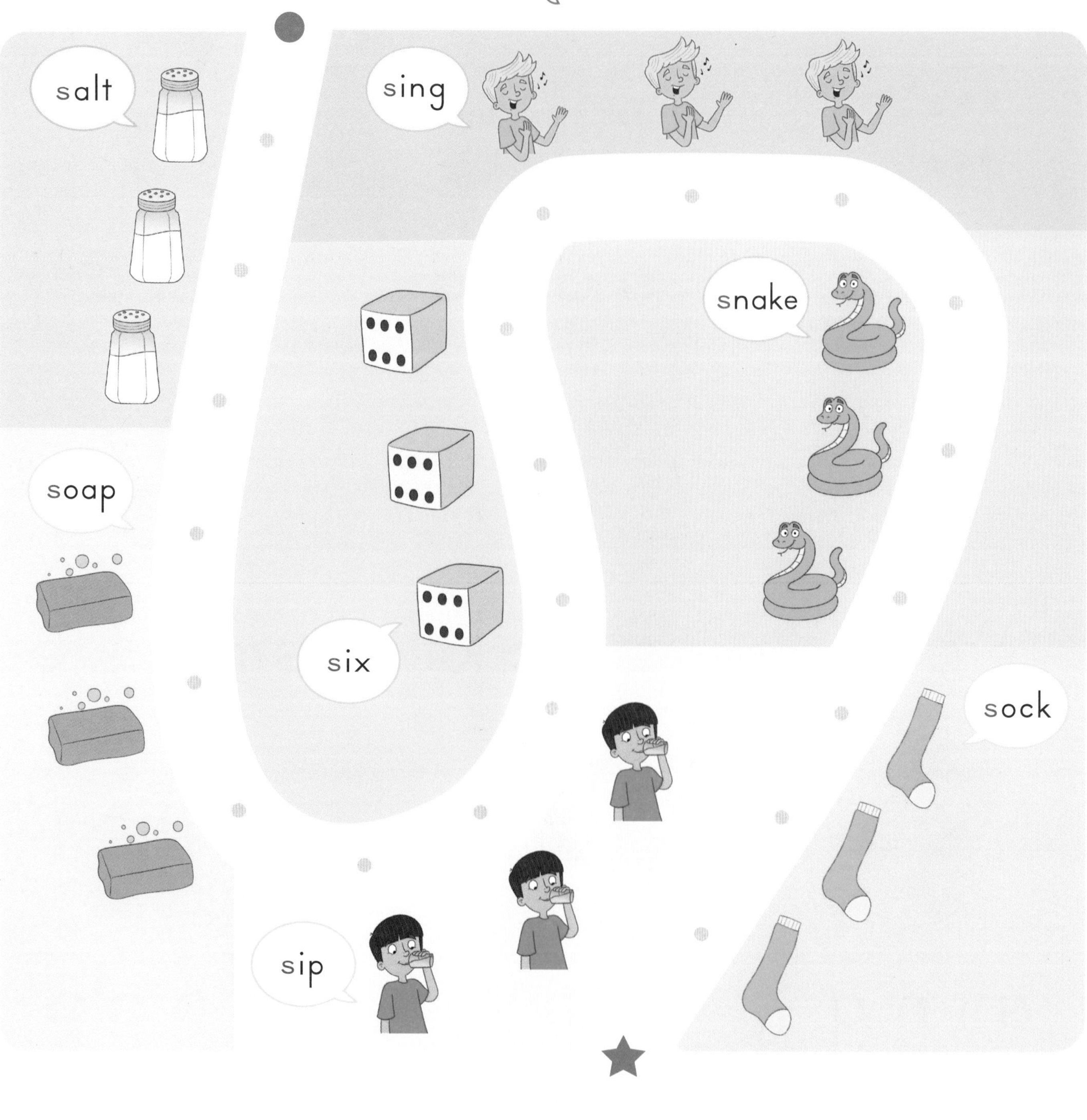

a b c d e f g h i j k l m n o p q r s t u v w x y z

Consonant Sounds

The "n" Sound

Name Date / /

To parents/guardians: It can be easy to confuse the "n" and "m" sounds. Listen carefully to be sure your child is saying "n."

■ Say the word represented by the picture out loud. Then circle the letter that makes the "n" sound at the beginning of the word.

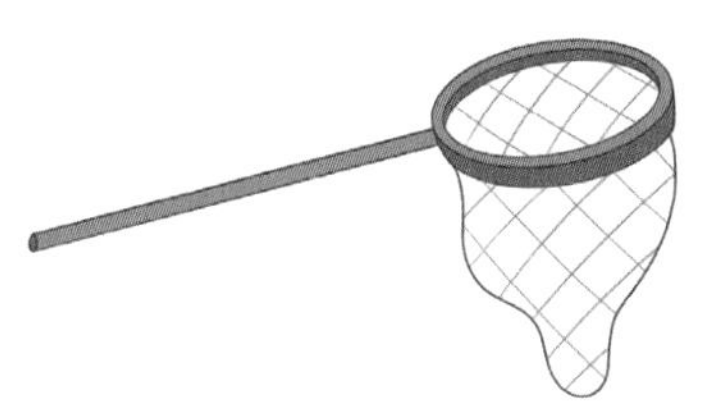

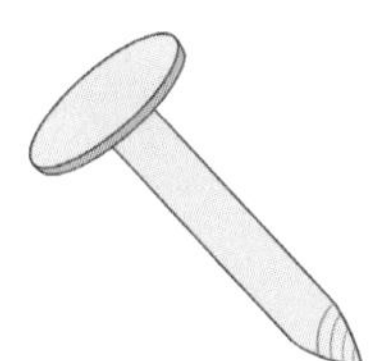

net nine nail

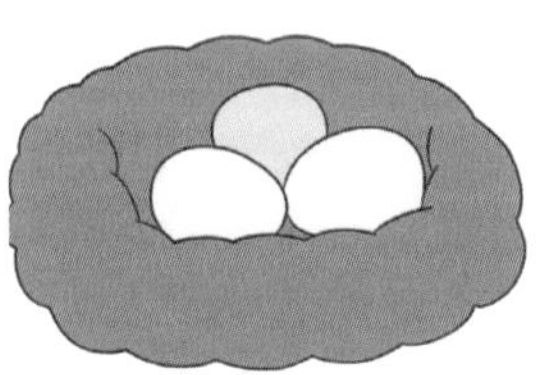

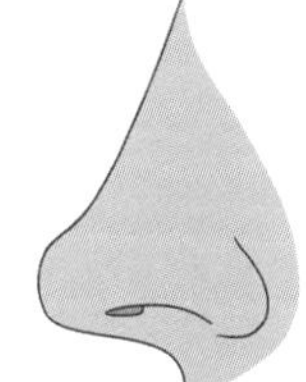

nest nose neck

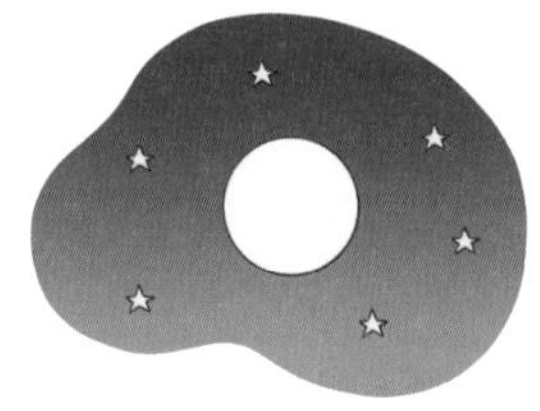

new nurse night

a b c d e f g h i j k l m n o p q r s t u v w x y z

■ Draw a line along the path from the dot (●) to the star (★).
Each time you pass an image, (say) the word out loud.

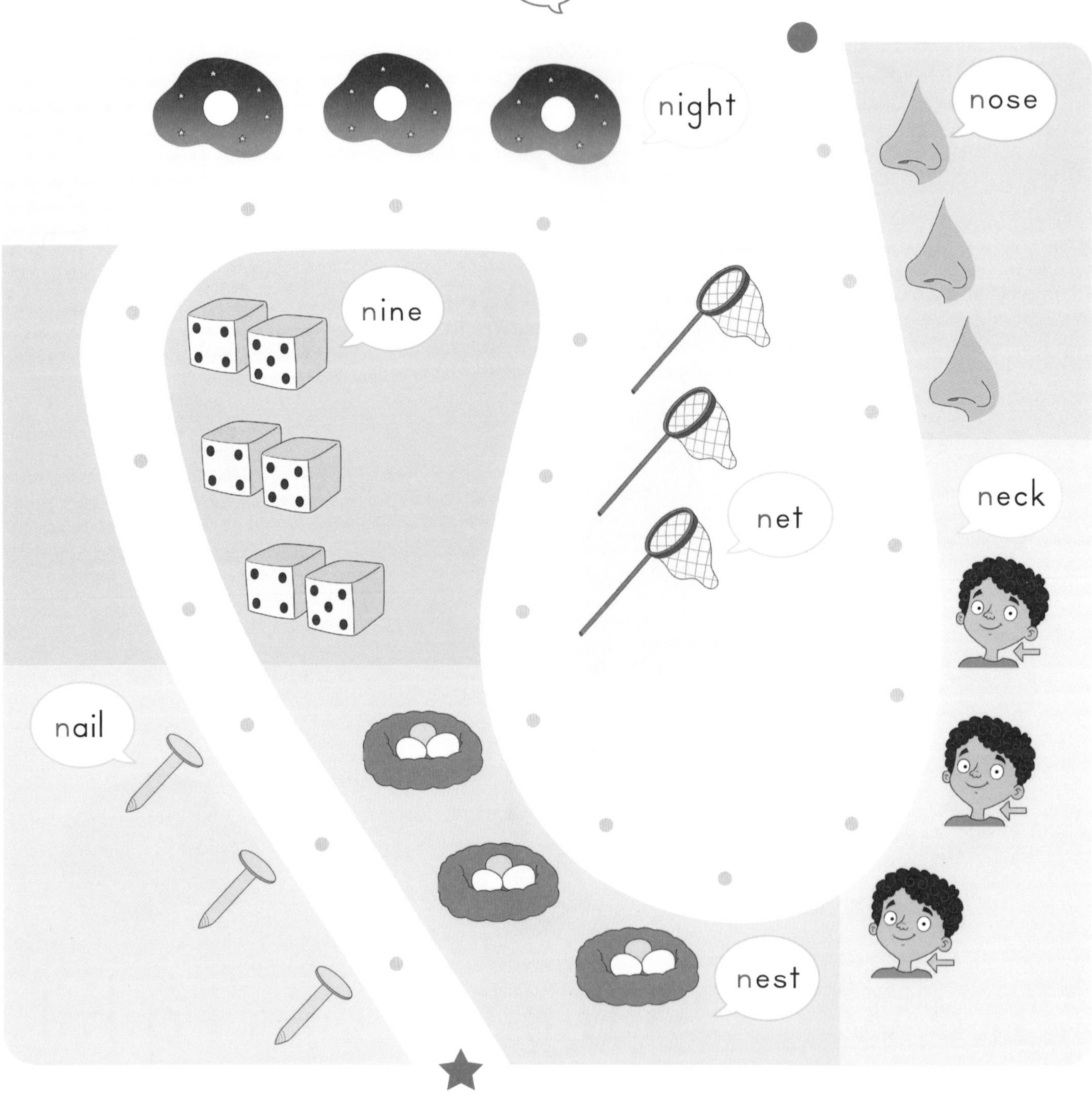

a b c d e f g h i j k l m n o p q r s t u v w x y z

17 Consonant Sounds

The "l" Sound

Name Date / /

To parents/guardians: For extra practice, encourage your child to think of other words that begin with the "l" sound.

■ Say the word represented by the picture out loud. Then circle the letter that makes the "l" sound at the beginning of the word.

lion leg lid

lips last lamp

lock lake lawn

a b c d e f g h i j k l m n o p q r s t u v w x y z

■ Draw a line along the path from the dot (●) to the star (★).
Each time you pass an image, (say) the word out loud.

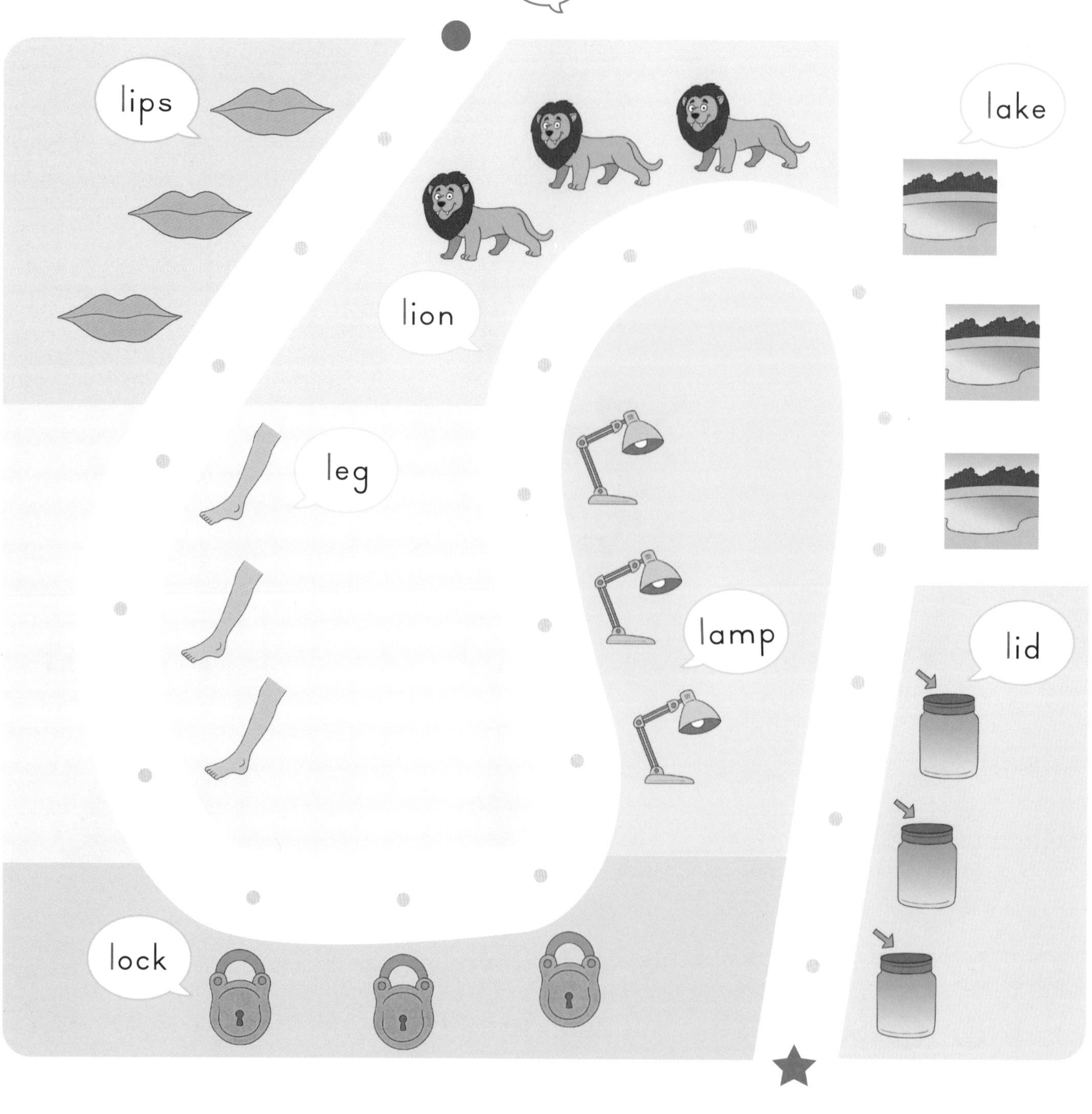

a b c d e f g h i j k l m n o p q r s t u v w x y z

18 Consonant Review

The "s", "n", and "l" Sounds

Name

Date / /

To parents/guardians: In this section, your child will review three letter sounds together. Make sure your child says each word out loud correctly to reinforce the letter sounds.

■ Say the word represented by the picture out loud. Then write in the missing letter.

s i p

a l t

i x

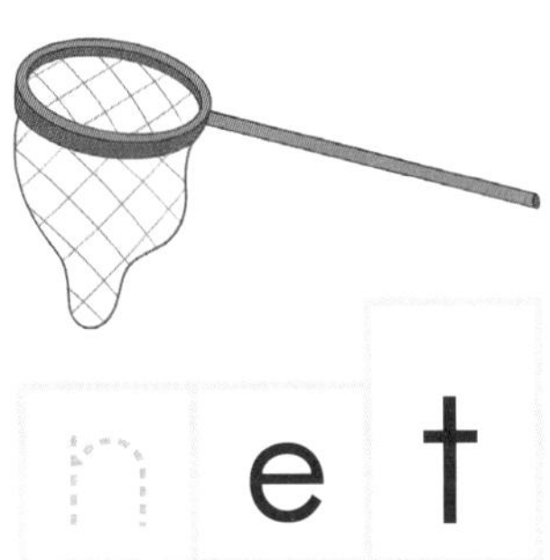

n e t

e w

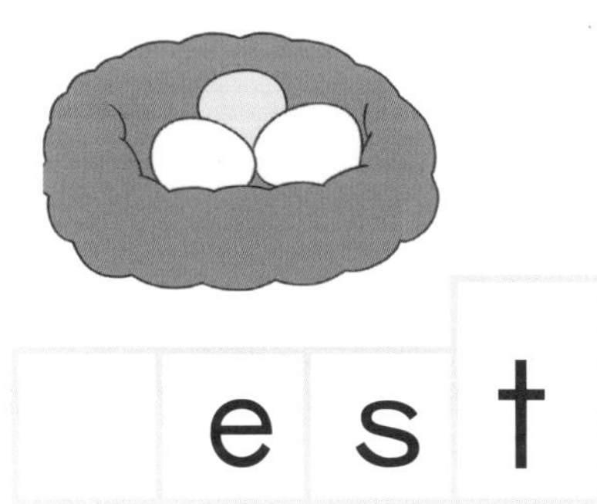

e s t

l i p s

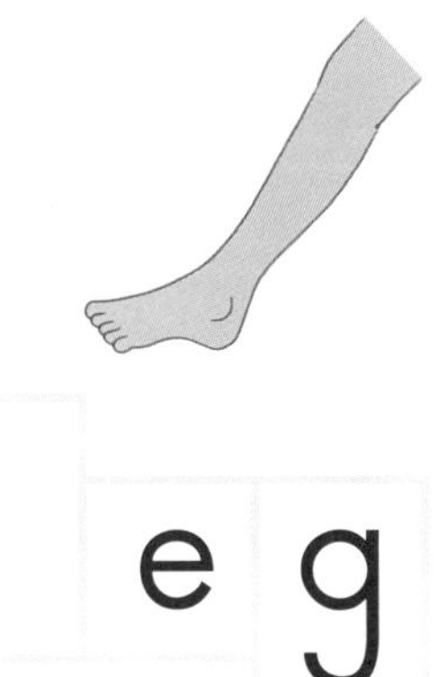

e g

i d

a	b	c	d	e	f	g	h	i	j	k	l	m	n	o	p	q	r	s	t	u	v	w	x	y	z

■ Trace each path from dot (●) to star (★) by following the words that begin with the same letter sound. Say each word as you go.

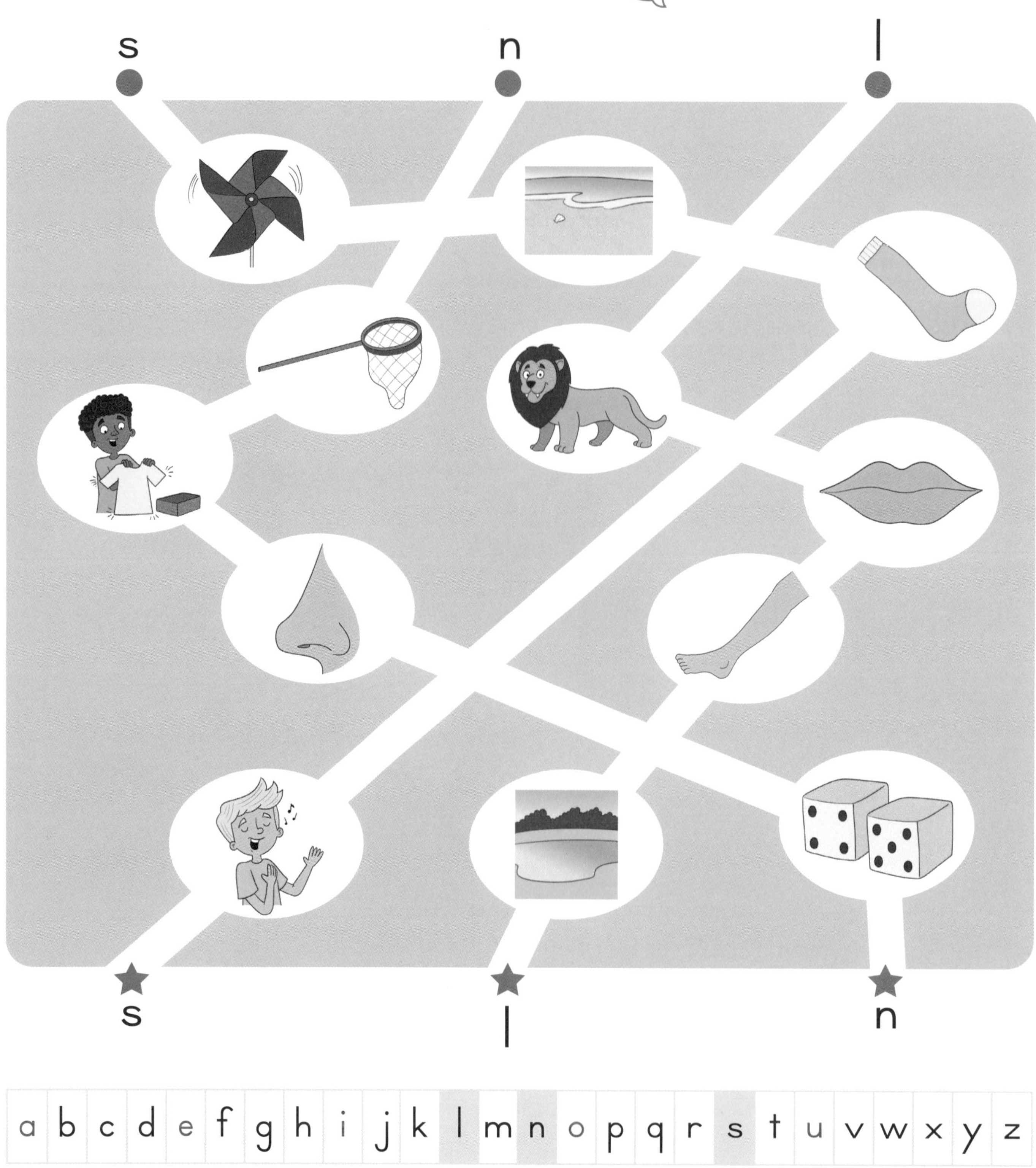

a	b	c	d	e	f	g	h	i	j	k	l	m	n	o	p	q	r	s	t	u	v	w	x	y	z

19 Consonant Sounds

The "f" Sound

Name

Date / /

To parents/guardians: It can be easy to confuse the "f" and "v" sounds. Listen carefully to be sure your child is saying "f."

■ Say the word represented by the picture out loud. Then circle the letter that makes the "f" sound at the beginning of the word.

fish

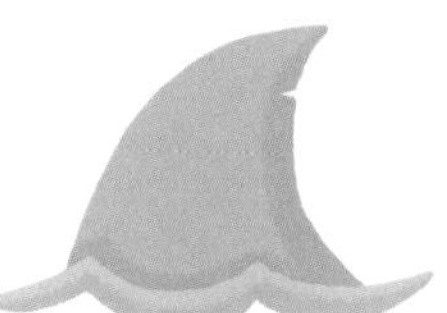

fin

fan

flag

frog

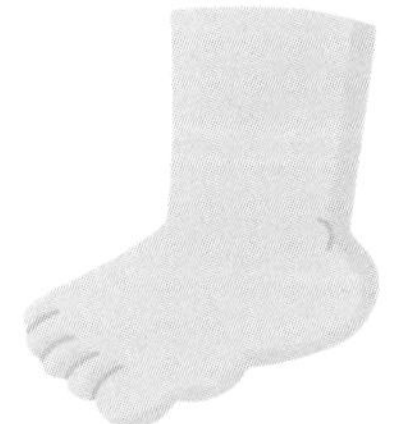

foot

fork

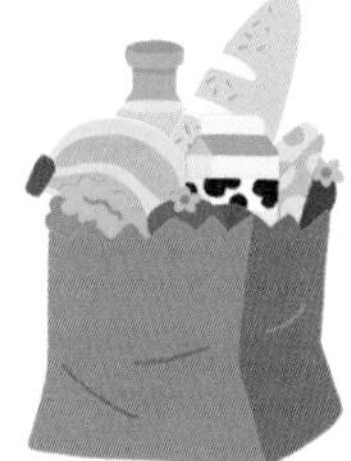

food

a b c d e f g h i j k l m n o p q r s t u v w x y z

- Draw a line along the path from the dot (●) to the star (★).
  Each time you pass an image, say the word out loud.

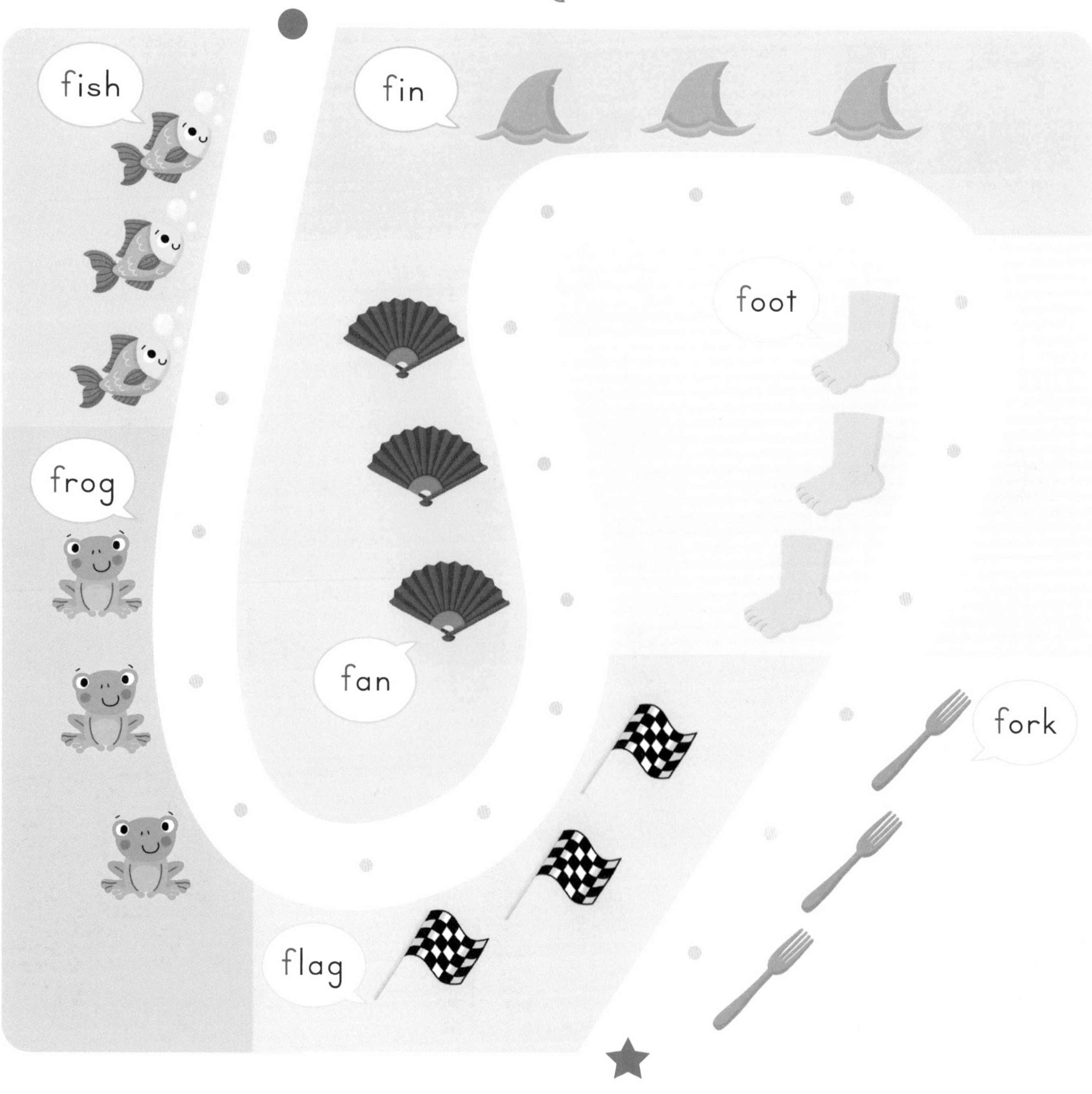

a b c d e f g h i j k l m n o p q r s t u v w x y z

Consonant Sounds

The "r" Sound

Name Date / /

To parents/guardians: Please note that for many children, the ability to pronounce the "r" sound often comes later in development. Give your child a lot of praise for their effort.

■ Say the word represented by the picture out loud. Then circle the letter that makes the "r" sound at the beginning of the word.

red

rope

rake

ring

rabbit

river

robot

rain

rose

a b c d e f g h i j k l m n o p q r s t u v w x y z

■ Draw a line along the path from the dot (●) to the star (★).
Each time you pass an image, say the word out loud.

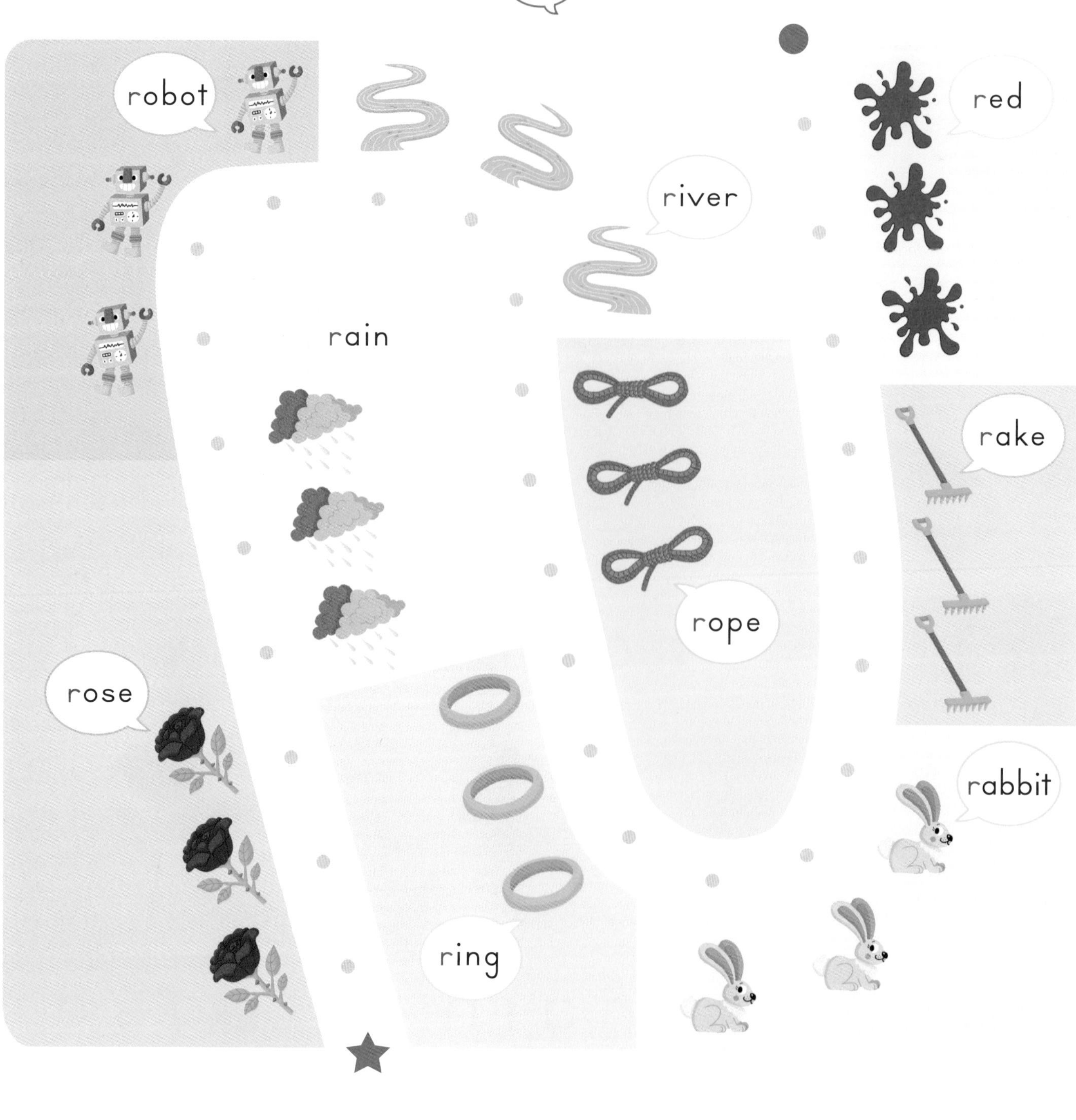

a	b	c	d	e	f	g	h	i	j	k	l	m	n	o	p	q	r	s	t	u	v	w	x	y	z

Consonant Sounds

The "h" Sound

Name

Date

/ /

To parents/guardians: Practice the "h" sound with your child. The "h" sound may be tricky because, in American English, the letter name *h* does not start with the "h" sound.

■ Say the word represented by the picture out loud. Then circle the letter that makes the "h" sound at the beginning of the word.

hug

hay

hit

horn

heart

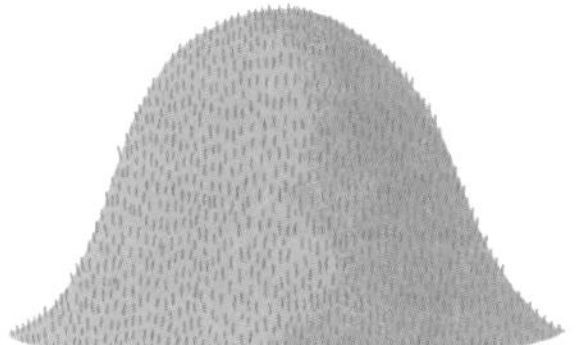

hill

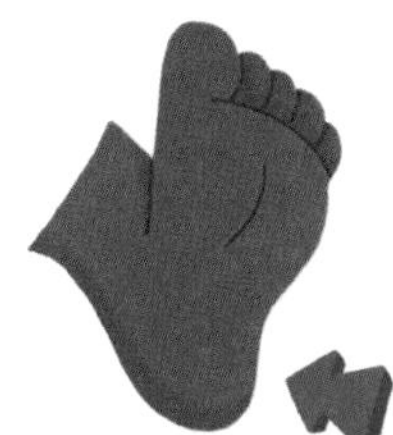

heel

horse

head

a b c d e f g h i j k l m n o p q r s t u v w x y z

■ Draw a line along the path from the dot (●) to the star (★).
Each time you pass an image, say the word out loud.

a b c d e f g h i j k l m n o p q r s t u v w x y z

Consonant Review

The "f", "r", and "h" Sounds

Name Date / /

To parents/guardians: In this section, your child will review three letter sounds together. Make sure your child says each word out loud correctly to reinforce the letter sounds.

■ Say the word represented by the picture out loud. Then write in the missing letter.

f i s h   a n   o r k

r a k e   i n g   o p e

h u g   e a r t   o r n

a b c d e f g h i j k l m n o p q r s t u v w x y z

■ Trace each path from dot (●) to star (★) by following the words that begin with the same letter sound. (Say) each word as you go.

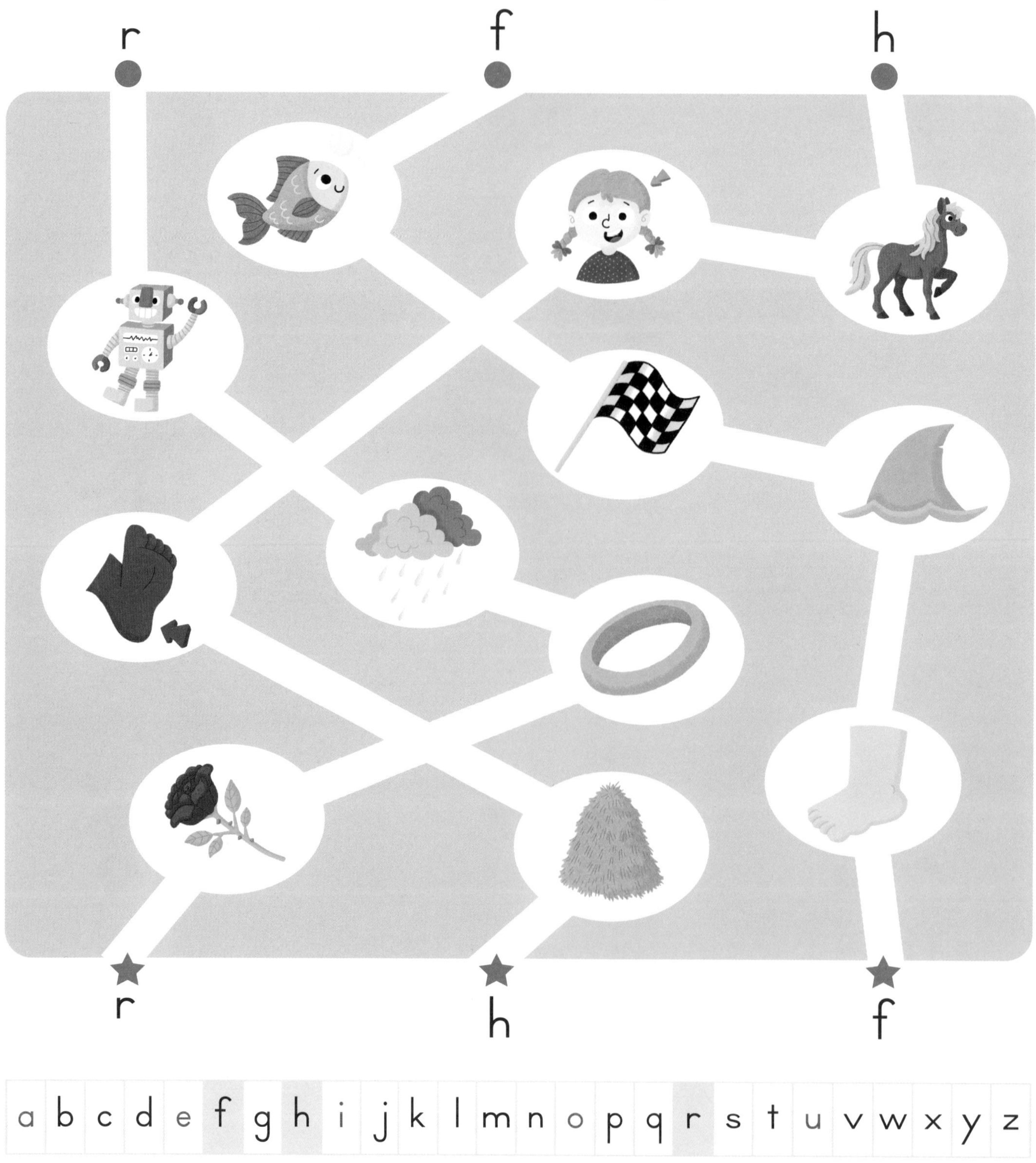

a b c d e f g h i j k l m n o p q r s t u v w x y z

Consonant Sounds

The "w" Sound

Name Date / /

To parents/guardians: Practice the "w" sound with your child. The "w" sound may be tricky because, in American English, the letter name *w* does not contain the "w" sound.

■ Say the word represented by the picture out loud. Then circle the letter that makes the "w" sound at the beginning of the word.

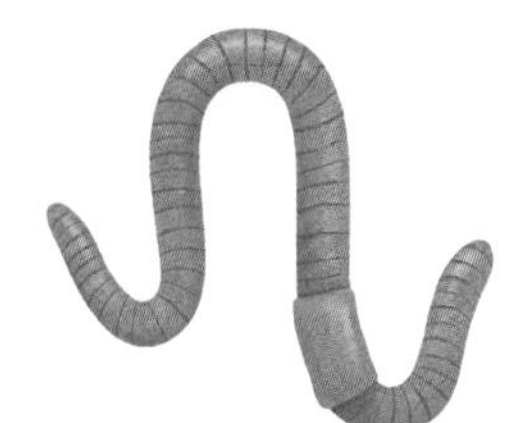

web worm wind

water wing wig

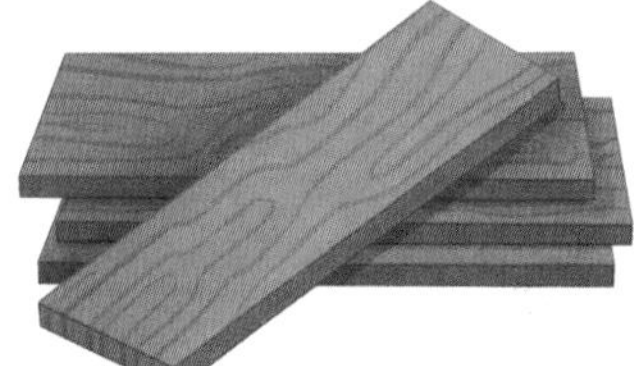

wall wood watch

a b c d e f g h i j k l m n o p q r s t u v w x y z

■ Draw a line along the path from the dot (●) to the star (★).
Each time you pass an image, (say) the word out loud.

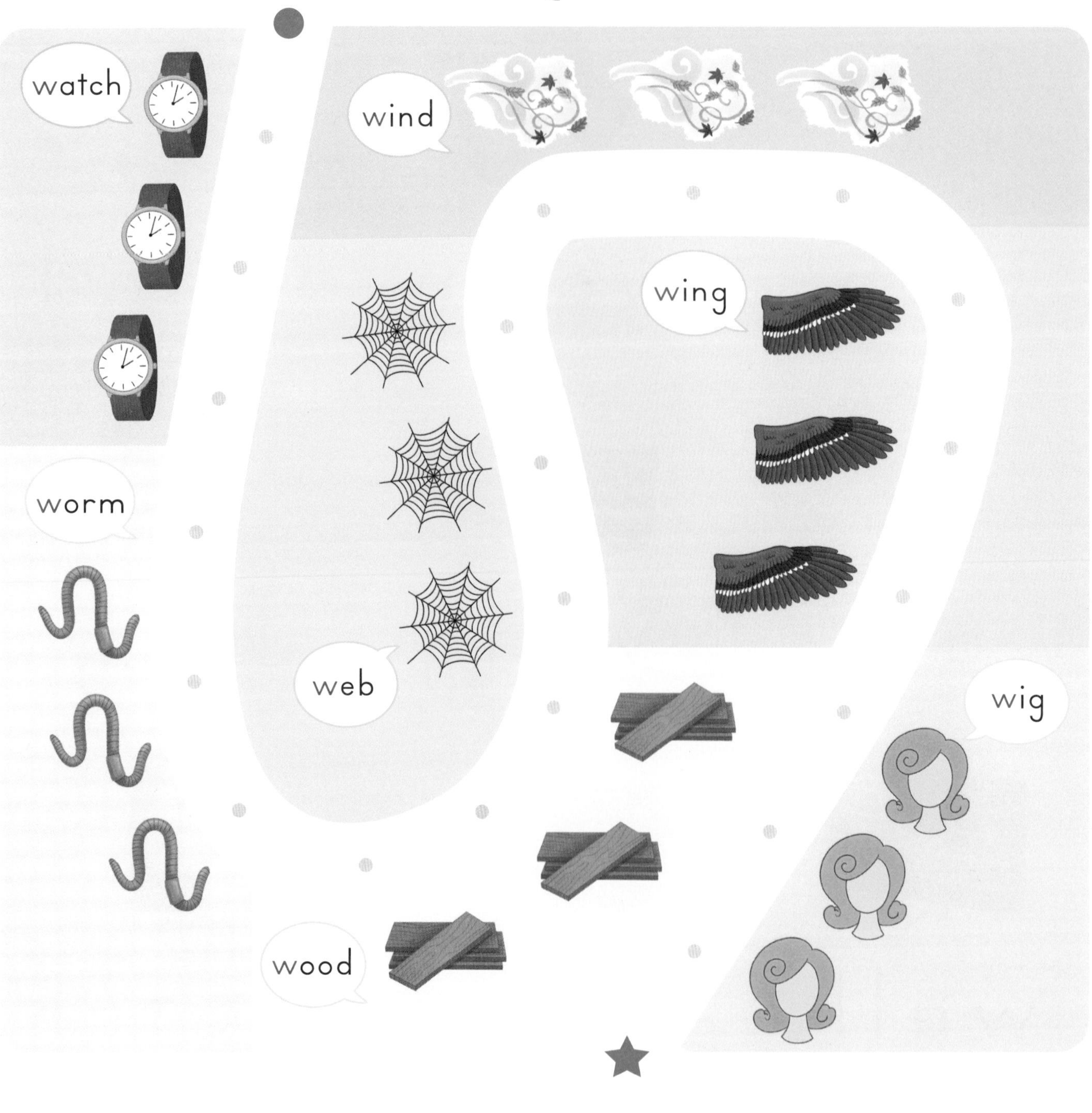

a b c d e f g h i j k l m n o p q r s t u v w x y z

Consonant Sounds

The "x" Sound

Name

Date

/ /

To parents/guardians: Familiar words that begin with *x* are relatively uncommon, so this section includes familiar words that either begin or end with *x*. The last two words are familiar words that begin with *x* and demonstrate the variety of sounds *x* can make.

■ Say the word represented by the picture out loud. Then circle the letter "x" in each word.

ox

six

box

mix

wax

fox

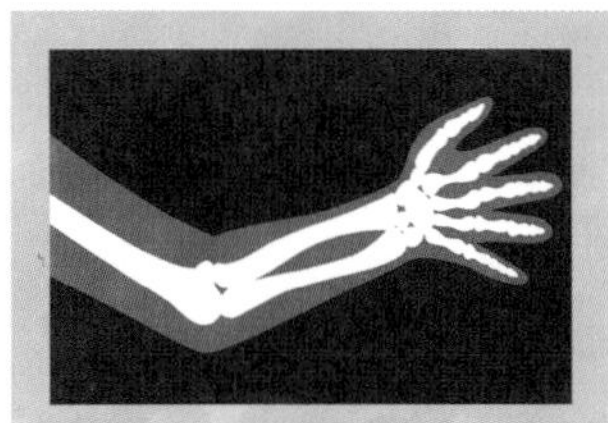

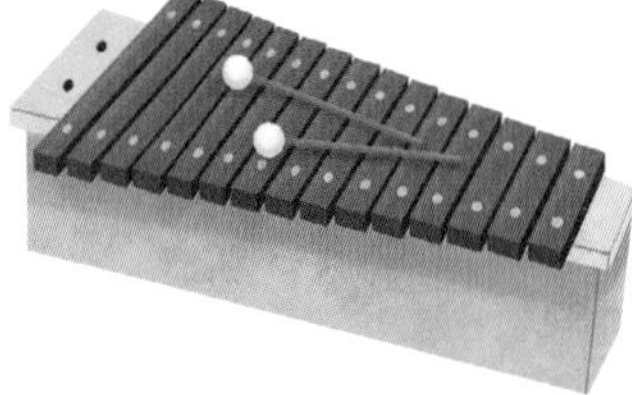

x-ray

xylophone

a b c d e f g h i j k l m n o p q r s t u v w x y z

■ Draw a line along the path from the dot (●) to the star (★).
Each time you pass an image, say the word out loud.

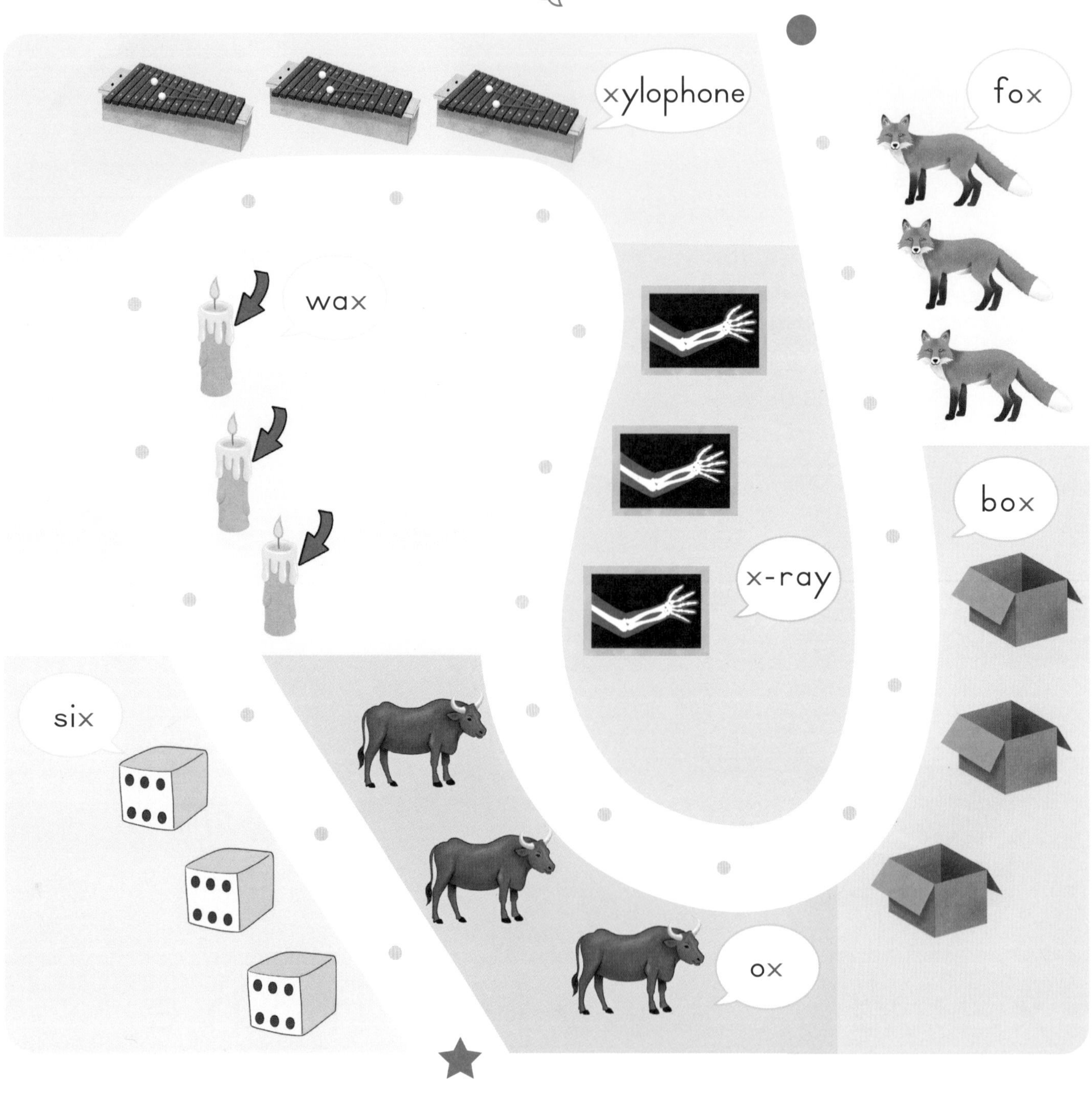

a b c d e f g h i j k l m n o p q r s t u v w x y z

Consonant Sounds

The "z" Sound

Name　　　　　　Date　　/　　/

To parents/guardians: Throughout this book, it is important that you encourage your child to say each word out loud. This will help your child learn the relationships between letters and sounds.

■ Say the word represented by the picture out loud. Then circle the letter that makes the "z" sound at the beginning of the word.

zebra

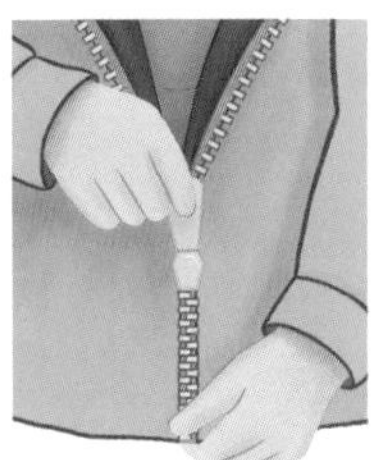

zip

zoom

zoo

zero

zipper

zigzag

zap

a b c d e f g h i j k l m n o p q r s t u v w x y z

■ Draw a line along the path from the dot (●) to the star (★).
Each time you pass an image, say the word out loud.

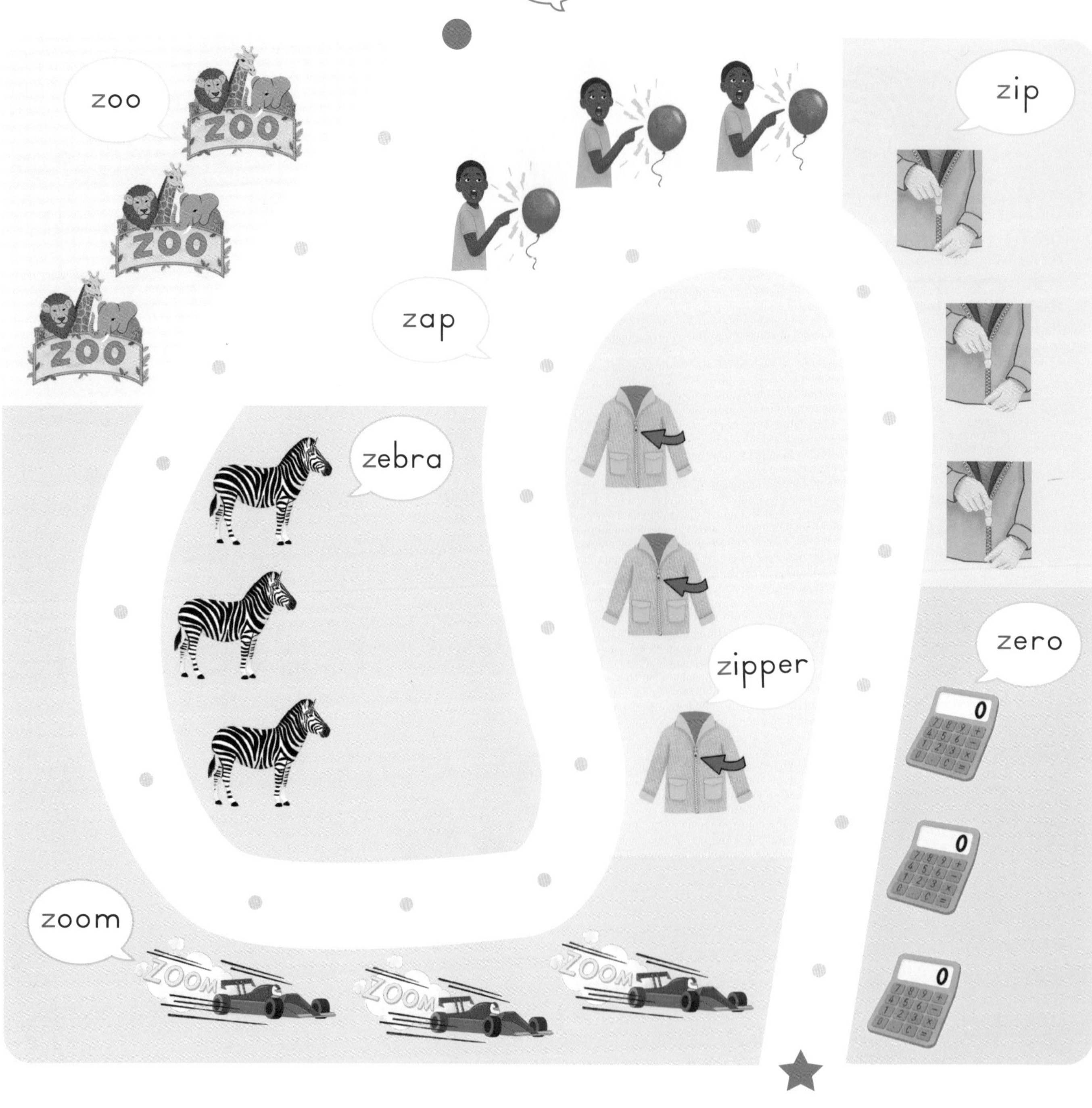

a b c d e f g h i j k l m n o p q r s t u v w x y z

26 Consonant Review

The "w", "x", and "z" Sounds

Name

Date / /

To parents/guardians: In this section, your child will review three letter sounds together. Make sure your child says each word out loud correctly to reinforce the letter sounds.

■ Say the word represented by the picture out loud. Then write in the missing letter.

w a t e r   o o d   e b

f o x   y l o p h o n e

z e b r a   o o   i p

a b c d e f g h i j k l m n o p q r s t u v w x y z

■ Trace each path from dot (●) to star (★) by following the words that begin with the same letter sound or that contain the letter x.

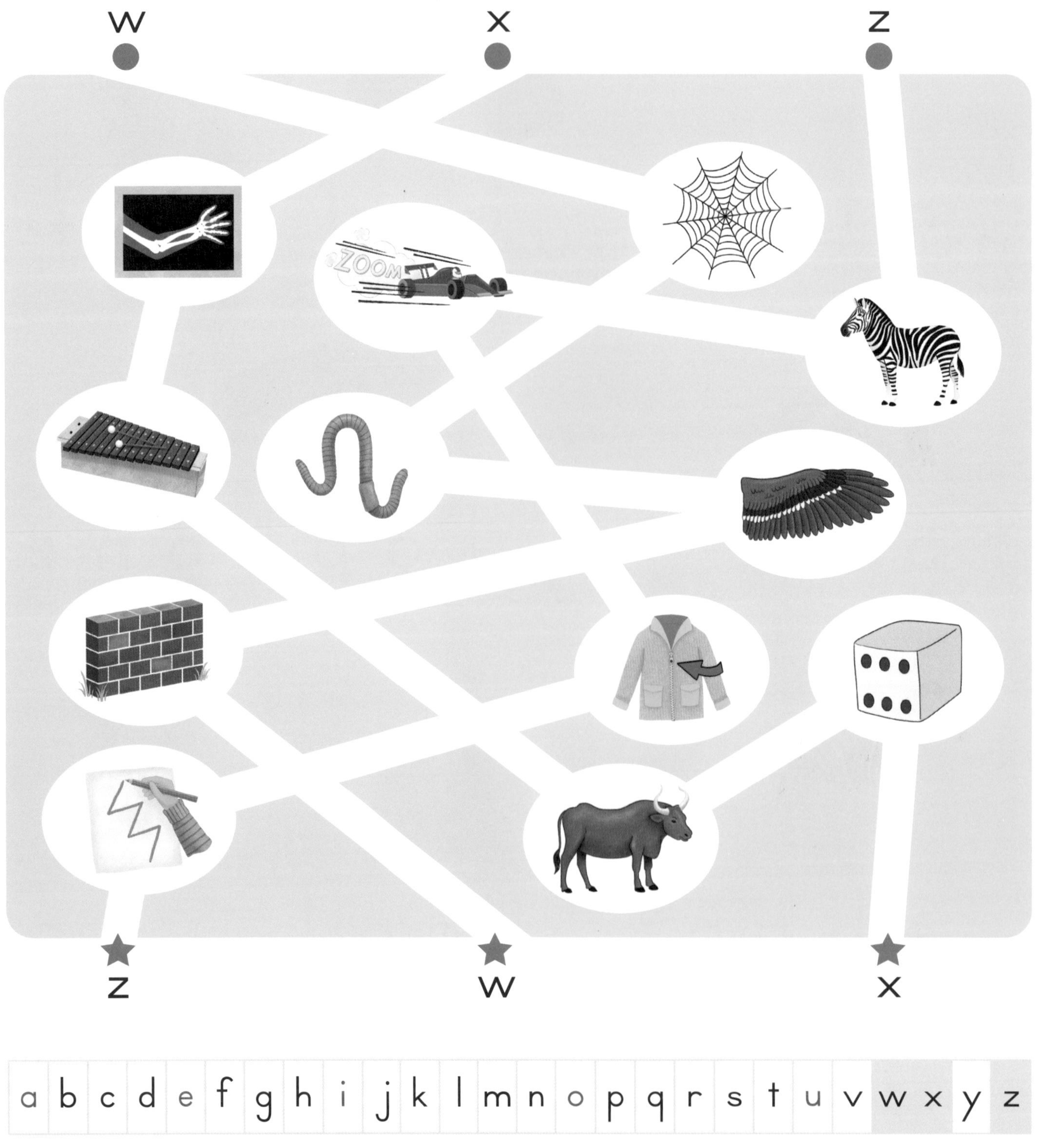

a b c d e f g h i j k l m n o p q r s t u v w x y z

Consonant Sounds

The "qu" Sound

Name

Date

/ /

To parents/guardians: As your child may already know, the consonant *q* is always followed by the vowel *u*. Sounds produced by two or more letters will be covered in more detail in the next book of this series.

■ Say the word represented by the picture out loud. Then circle the letters that make the "qu" sound at the beginning of the word.

queen

quick

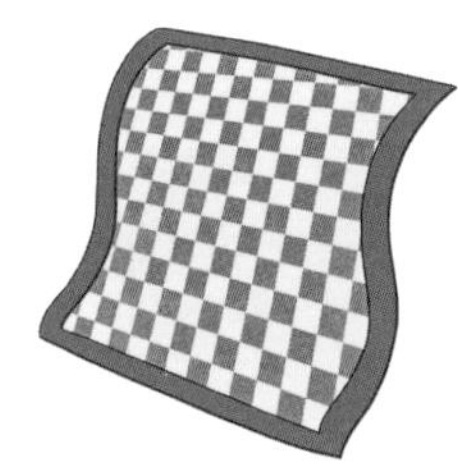

quilt

quiet

quarter

quail

question

quack

a b c d e f g h i j k l m n o p q r s t u v w x y z

■ Draw a line along the path from the dot (●) to the star (★). Each time you pass an image, say the word out loud.

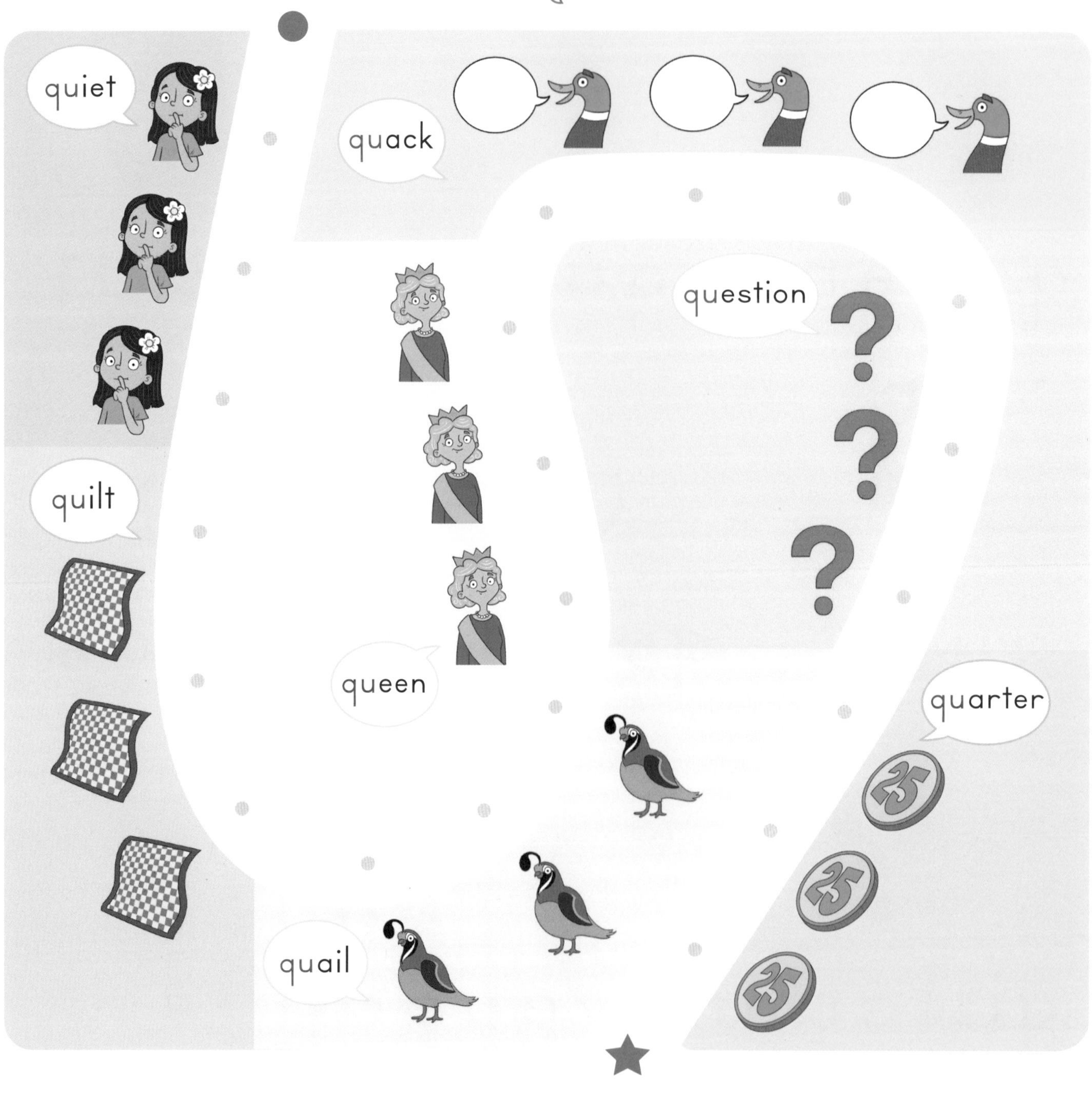

a b c d e f g h i j k l m n o p q r s t u v w x y z

28

Consonant Sounds

The "v" Sound

Name　　　　　　Date　/　/

To parents/guardians: It can be easy to confuse the "f" and "v" sounds. Listen carefully to be sure your child is saying "v."

■ Say the word represented by the picture out loud. Then circle the letter that makes the "v" sound at the beginning of the word.

van　veil　violin

vest　volcano　vine

village　vegetables

a b c d e f g h i j k l m n o p q r s t u v w x y z

■ Draw a line along the path from the dot (●) to the star (★). Each time you pass an image, say the word out loud.

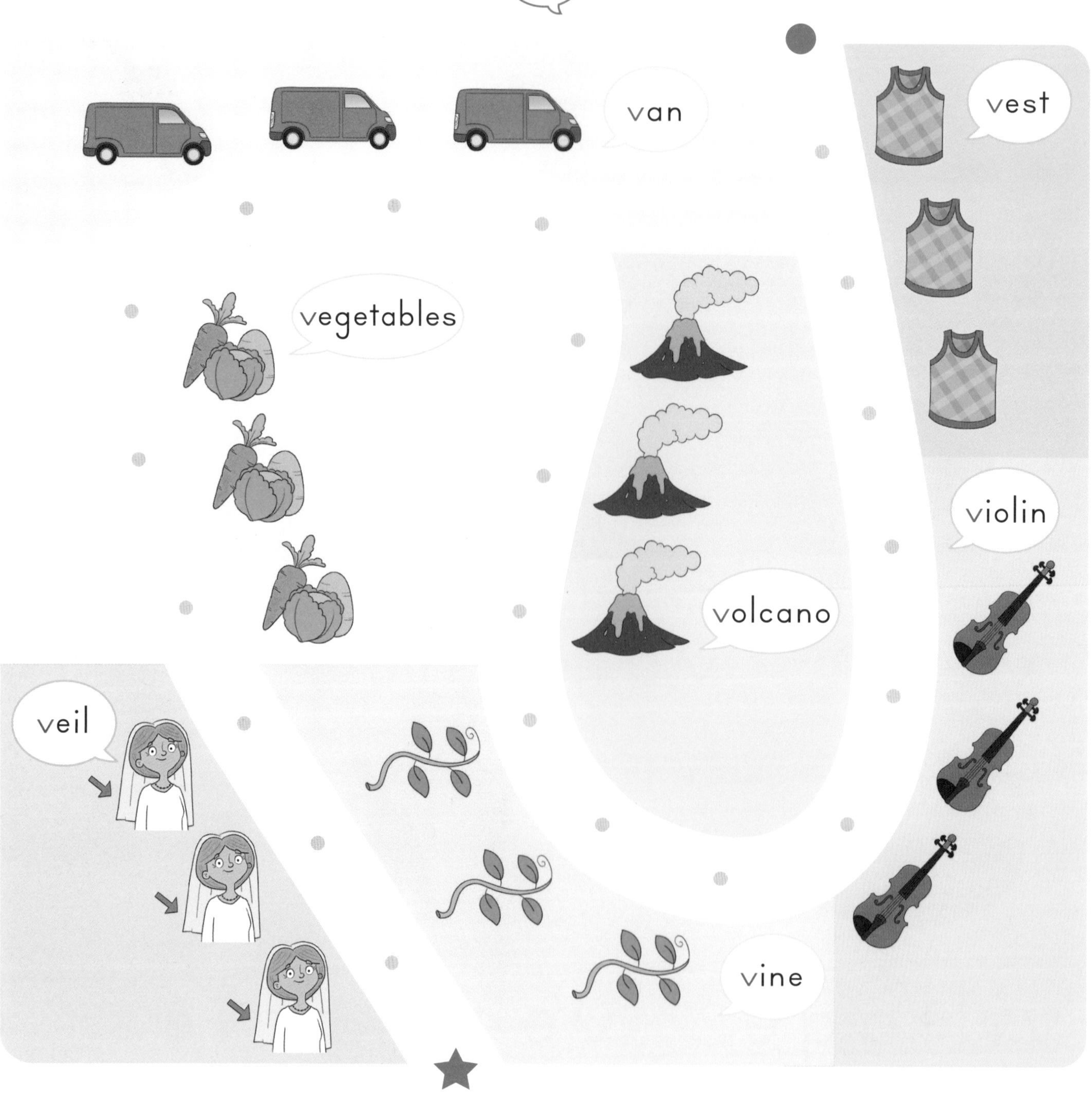

a b c d e f g h i j k l m n o p q r s t u v w x y z

Consonant Sounds

The "y" Sound

Name Date / /

To parents/guardians: On this page, your child will learn the sound of the letter *y* as a consonant sound. Your child might already know that *y* can also be a vowel, which will be addressed in the next book of this series.

■ Say the word represented by the picture out loud. Then circle the letter that makes the "y" sound at the beginning of the word.

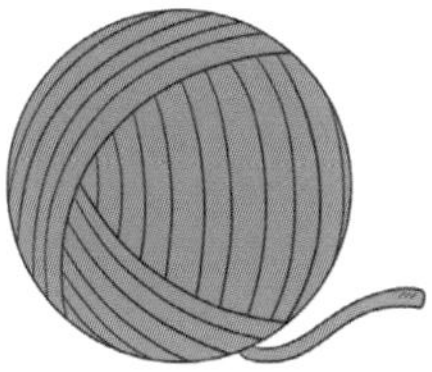

yarn  yell  yak

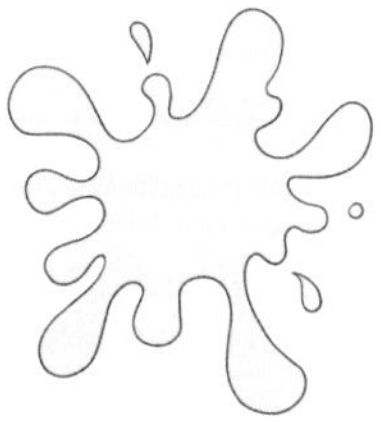

yellow  yes  yawn

YES

you  yummy 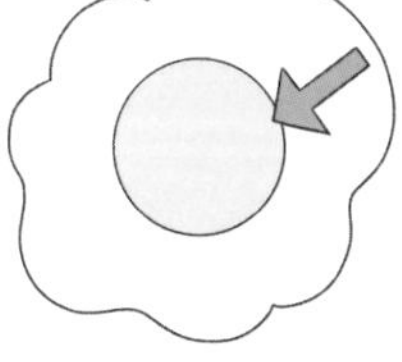 yolk

a b c d e f g h i j k l m n o p q r s t u v w x y z

■ Draw a line along the path from the dot (●) to the star (★).
Each time you pass an image, say the word out loud.

a b c d e f g h i j k l m n o p q r s t u v w x y z

Consonant Review

The “qu”, “v”, and “y” Sounds

Name Date / /

To parents/guardians: By this point, your child has almost finished the consonant section of this book. If your child has completed all the pages so far, offer them a lot of praise. You can say “Good job!” or place a sticker on the page as a reward.

■ Say the word represented by the picture out loud. Then write in the missing letter or letters.

q u e e n

a r t e r

v i o l i n

o l c a n o

y a k

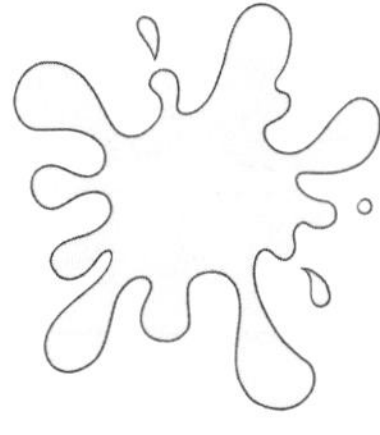

e l l o w

o l k

a b c d e f g h i j k l m n o p q r s t u v w x y z

■ Trace each path from dot (●) to star (★) by following the words that begin with the same letter sound. (Say) each word as you go.

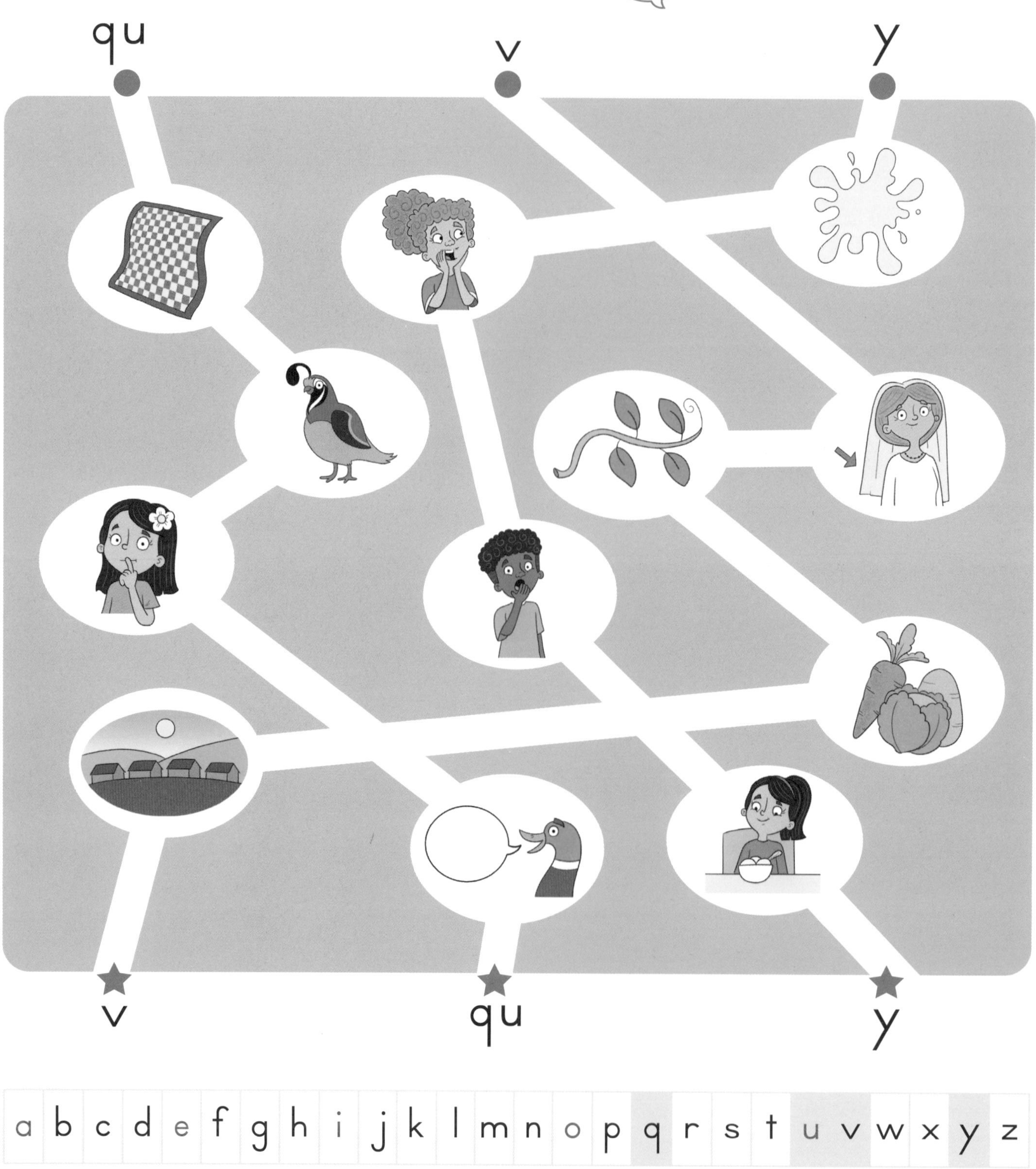

a b c d e f g h i j k l m n o p q r s t u v w x y z

31 Review

Consonant Sounds

Name

Date

/ /

To parents/guardians: In this section, your child will review consonant sounds. When learning consonant sounds for the first time, children often confuse similar-looking or similar-sounding letters. To support your child, watch for this particular kind of mistake.

■ Say the word represented by the picture out loud. Then circle the beginning letter of the word.

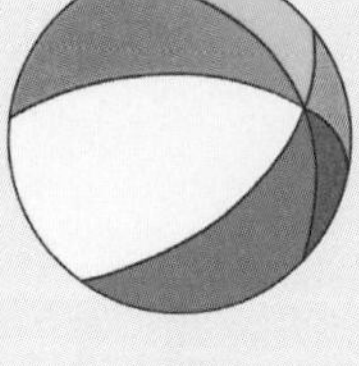

b p

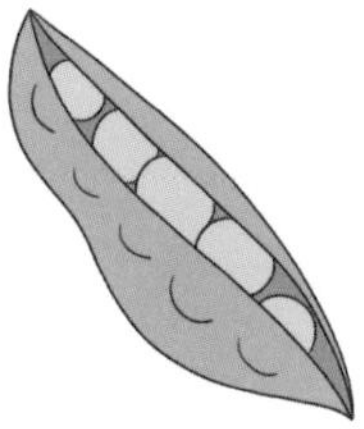

s p

d h

k d

k s

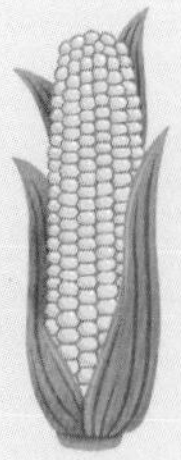

b c

c g

h p

qu j

g j

■ Say the word represented by the picture out loud.
Then circle the beginning letter of the word.

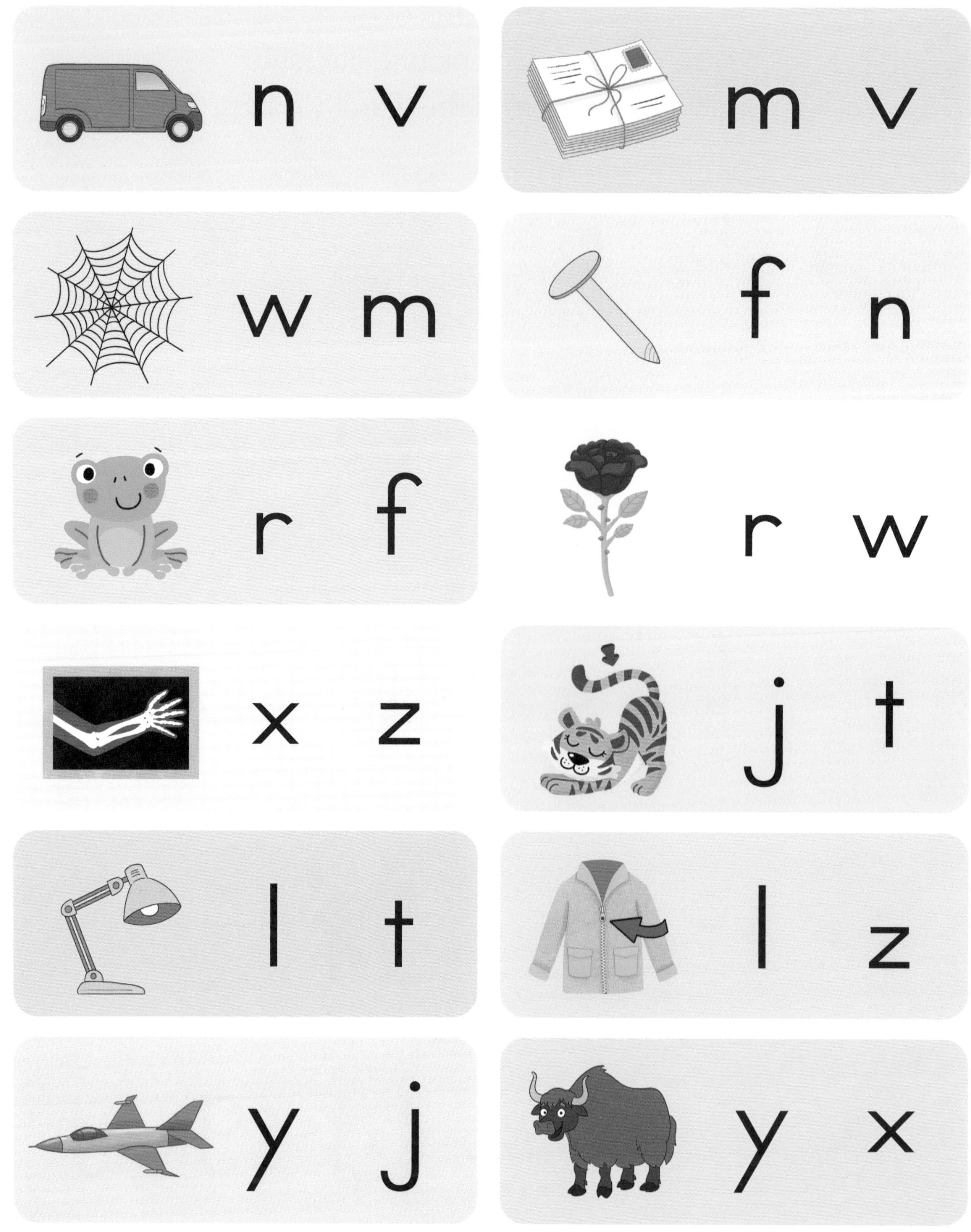

Introducing Vowels

Recognizing a, e, i, o, and u

Name

Date / /

To parents/guardians: In this section, your child is introduced to the vowels *a*, *e*, *i*, o, and *u*.

■ Color the picture using the key below.

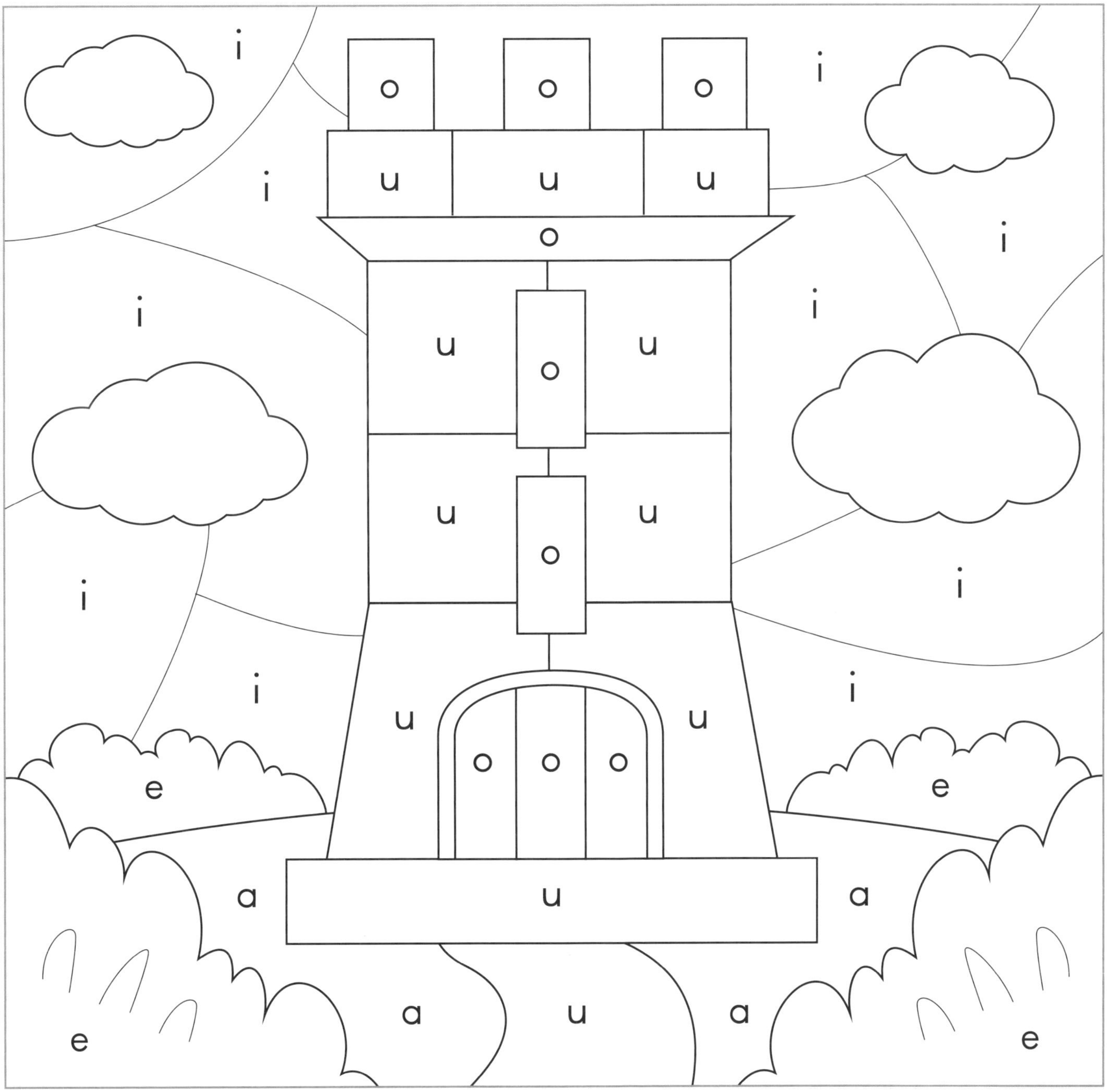

castle

a b c d e f g h i j k l m n o p q r s t u v w x y z

■ Color the picture using the key below.

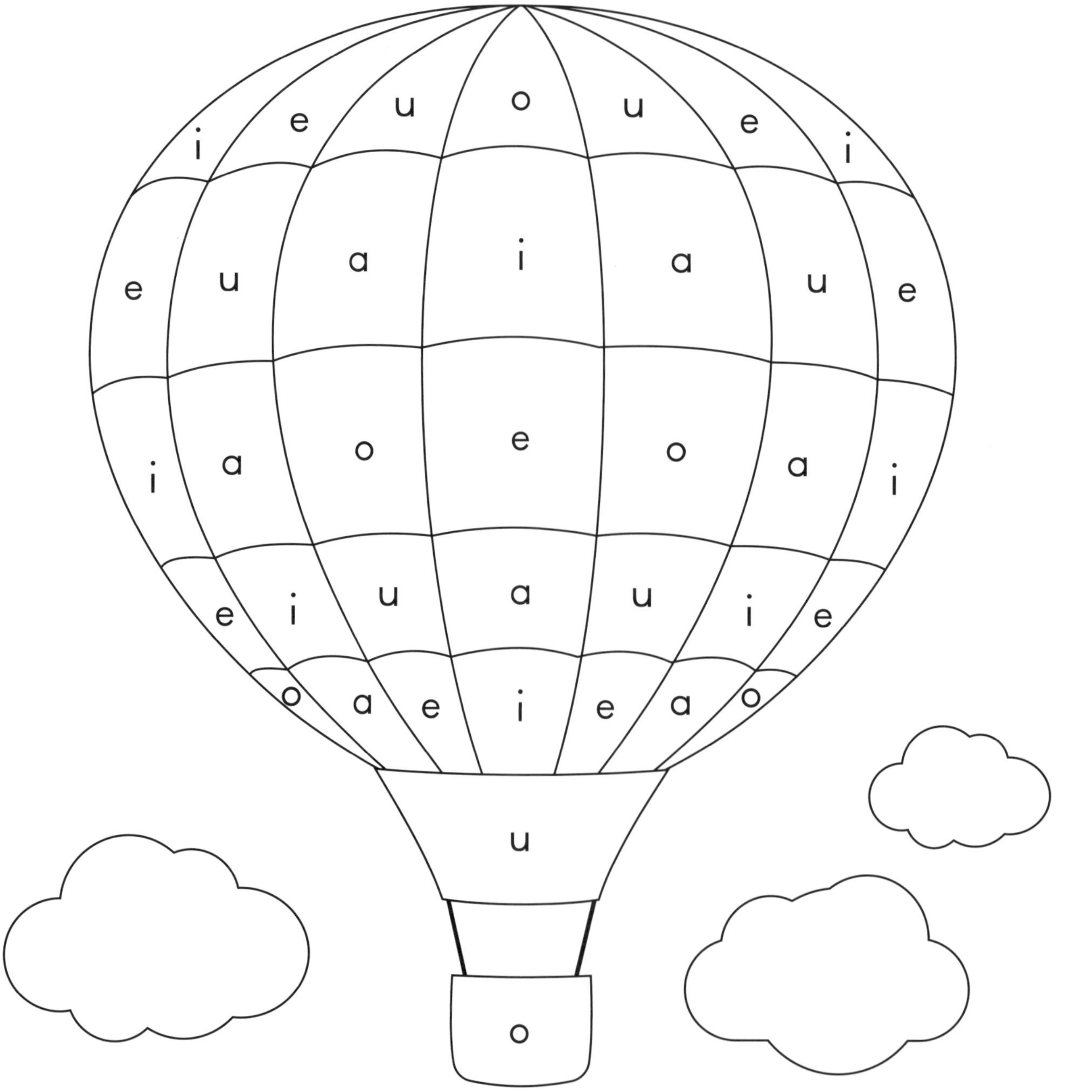

hot air balloon

a b c d e f g h i j k l m n o p q r s t u v w x y z

33

Introducing Vowels

Identifying the Vowels

Name

Date

/ /

To parents/guardians: In this section, your child is introduced to the idea of vowels as a separate group of letters from consonants.

■ Look for the vowels a, e, i, o, and u.
Color the apples with vowels yellow.
Color the apples with other letters red.

a b c d e f g h i j k l m n o p q r s t u v w x y z

■ Look for the vowels a, e, i, o, and u.
Color the shells with vowels pink.
Color the shells with other letters orange.

a	b	c	d	e	f	g	h	i	j	k	l	m	n	o	p	q	r	s	t	u	v	w	x	y	z

Vowel Sounds

The Short "a" Sound

Name

Date
/ /

To parents/guardians: From this page on your child will learn short vowel sounds. It is important for your child to say each word out loud several times. This will help them learn to identify the sound each short vowel makes.

■ Say the word represented by the picture out loud.
Then circle the letter that makes the short "a" sound.

WELCOME

c a t

h a t

m a t

10.00

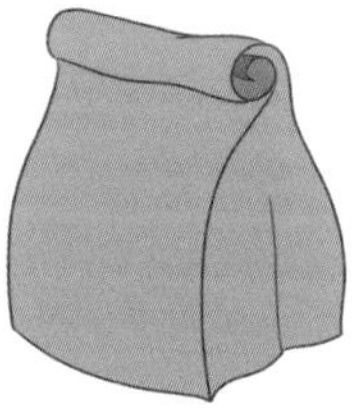

b a g

t a g

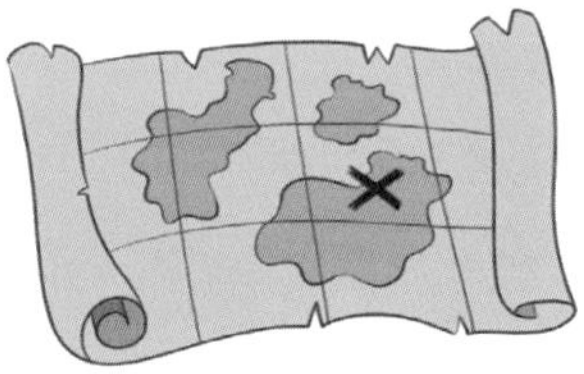

m a p

p a n

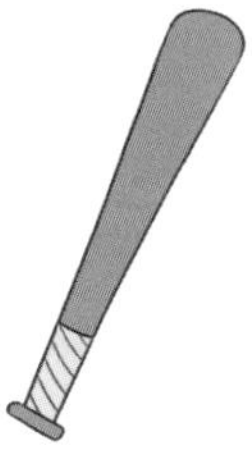

b a t

f a n

a b c d e f g h i j k l m n o p q r s t u v w x y z

To parents/guardians: On this page, your child will trace a path as they repeat words containing the short "a" sound.

■ Draw a line along the path from the dot (●) to the star (★). Each time you pass an image, say the word out loud.

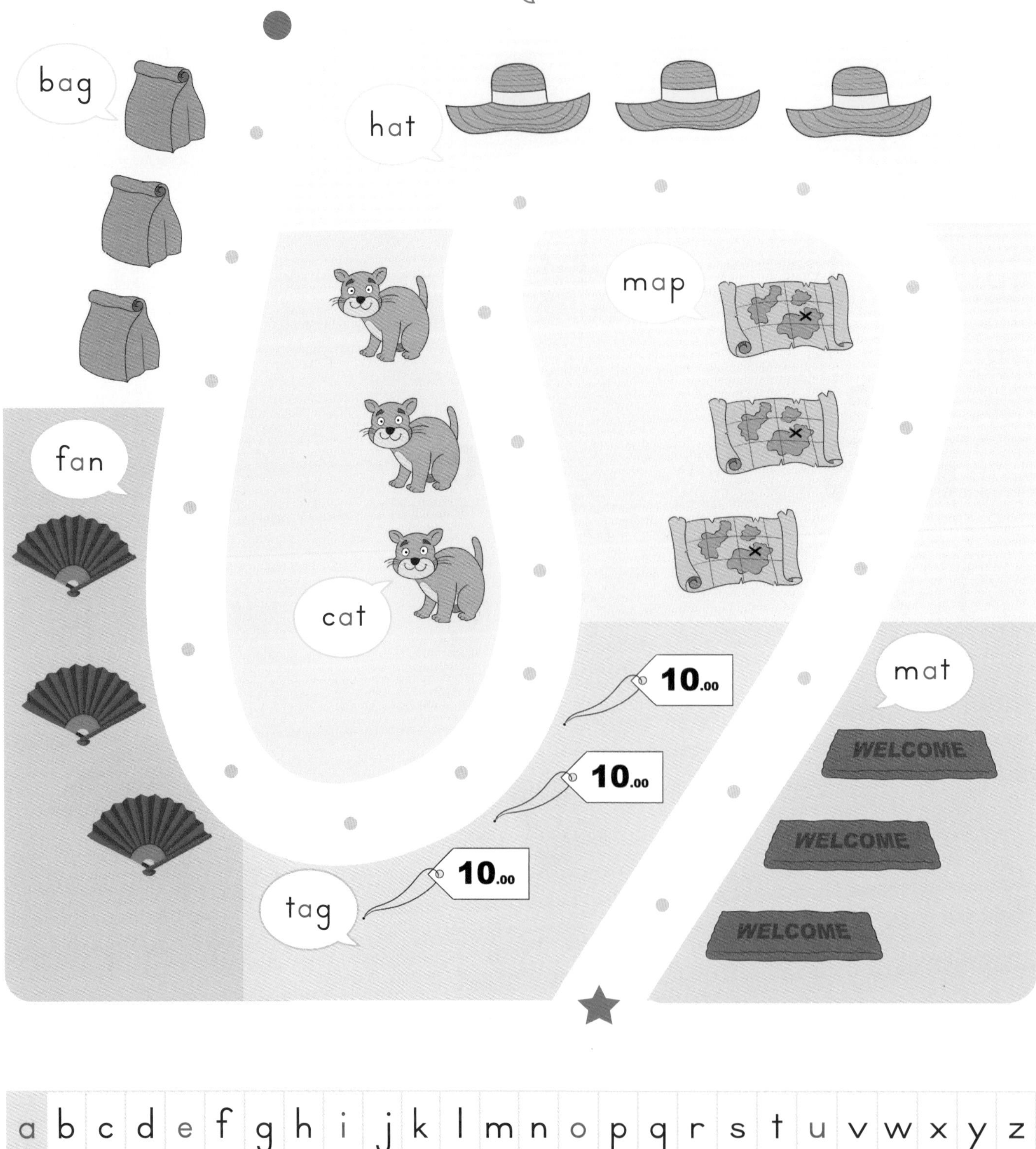

a b c d e f g h i j k l m n o p q r s t u v w x y z

Vowel Sounds

Recognizing the Short "a" Sound

Name

Date

/ /

To parents/guardians: If your child has trouble circling the right words, have them say all the words out loud again. Encourage them to listen for the two words in each row that rhyme.

■ Say the words represented by the pictures out loud.
Two words in each row have the short "a" sound. Circle them.

hat  bee 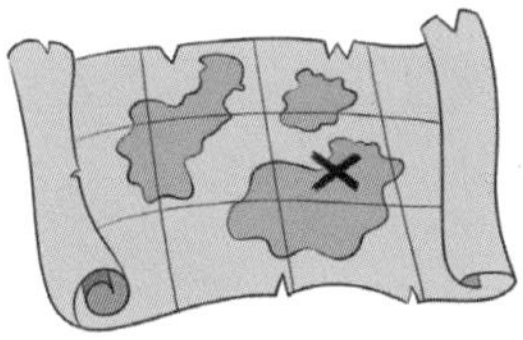 map

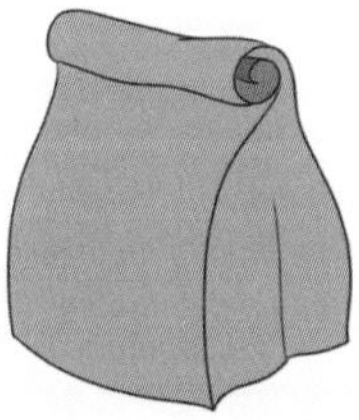

bag  pan 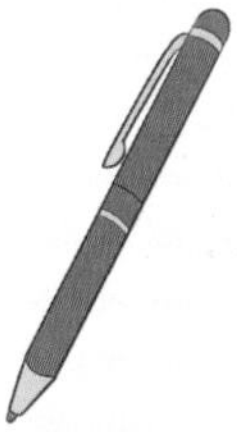 pen

book  fan  cat

a b c d e f g h i j k l m n o p q r s t u v w x y z

To parents/guardians: Here your child will distinguish between vowel sounds. It is important that you remind your child to say all the words out loud so they can hear the difference between the vowel sounds.

■ Say the words represented by the pictures out loud. One word in each group has the short "a" sound. Circle it.

a b c d e f g h i j k l m n o p q r s t u v w x y z

36 Vowel Sounds

The Short "e" Sound

Name

Date
/ /

To parents/guardians: It is important that your child says each word out loud so they can better hear the sound each vowel makes. Encourage your child to say the words on this page aloud several times.

■ Say the word represented by the picture out loud. Then circle the letter that makes the short "e" sound.

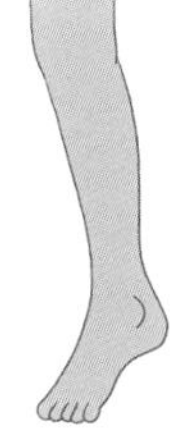

red hen leg

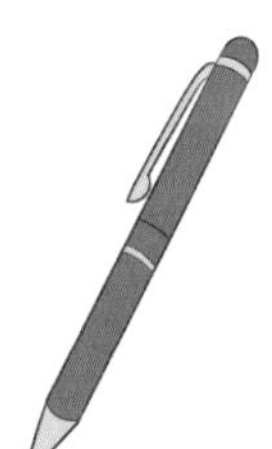

pen pet wet

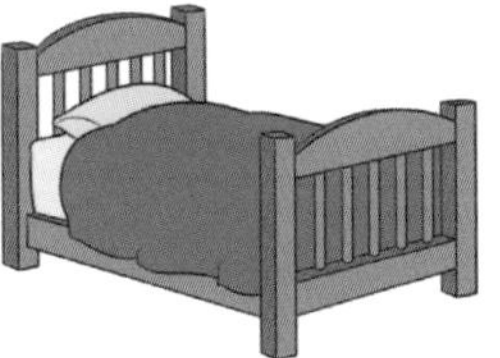

net den bed

a b c d e f g h i j k l m n o p q r s t u v w x y z

■ Draw a line along the path from the dot (●) to the star (★). Each time you pass an image, say the word out loud.

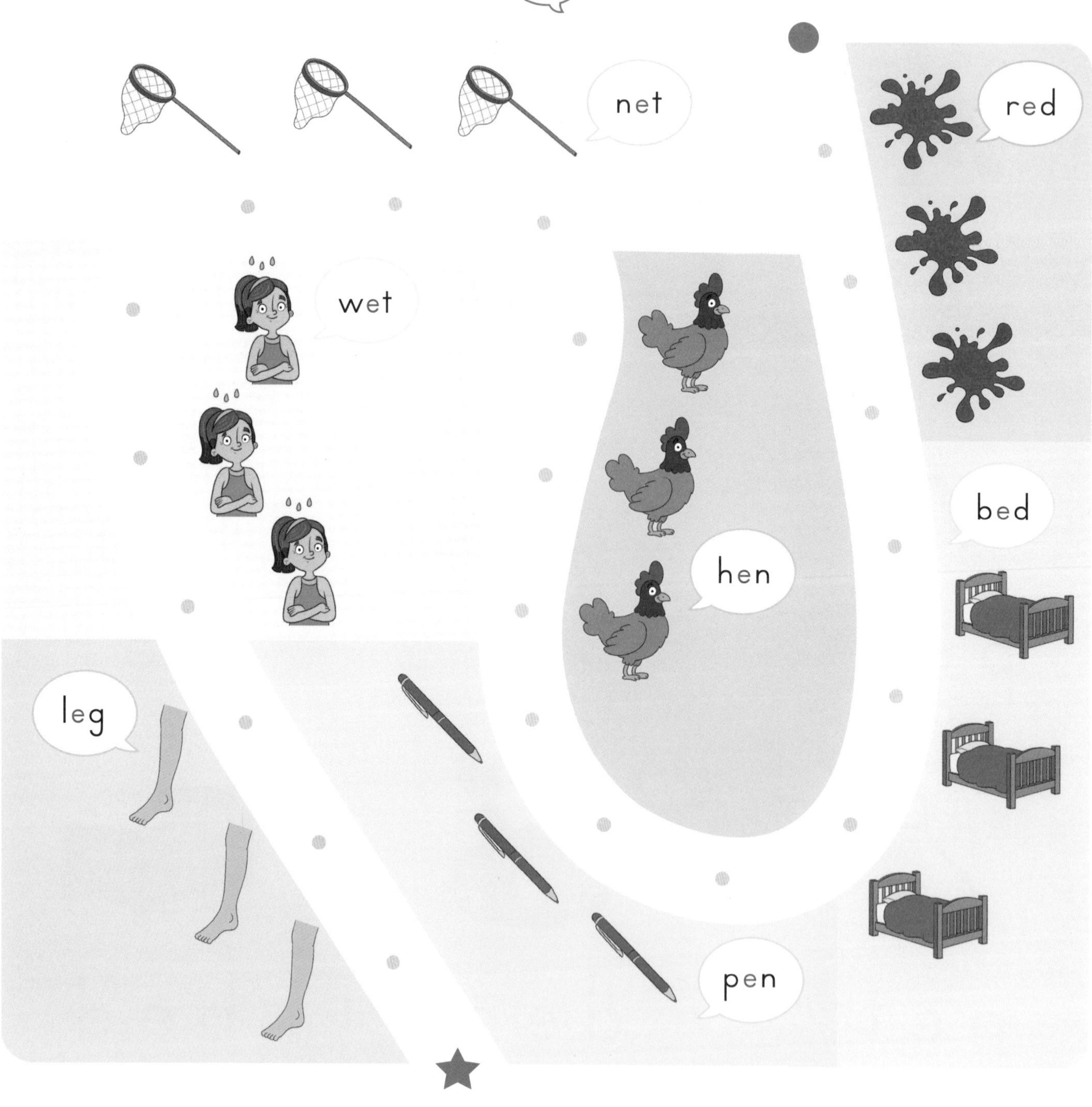

a b c d e f g h i j k l m n o p q r s t u v w x y z

Vowel Sounds

Recognizing the Short "e" Sound

Name

Date / /

To parents/guardians: For extra practice, have your child think of more words that contain the "short *e*" sound.

■ Say the words represented by the pictures out loud.
Two words in each row have the short "e" sound. Circle them.

red

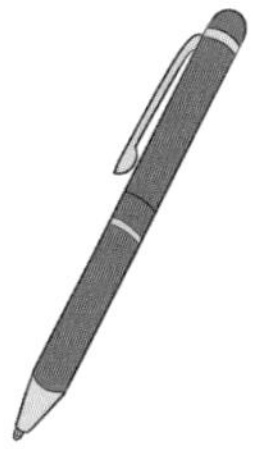

pen

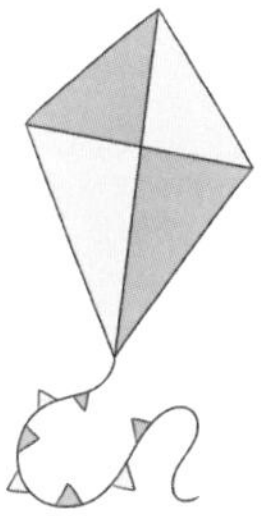

kite

wet

nail

hen

lock

pet

bed

a	b	c	d	e	f	g	h	i	j	k	l	m	n	o	p	q	r	s	t	u	v	w	x	y	z

■ Say the words represented by the pictures out loud.
One word in each group has the short "e" sound. Circle it.

a b c d e f g h i j k l m n o p q r s t u v w x y z

Vowel Sounds

The Short "i" Sound

Name Date / /

To parents/guardians: When a new short vowel is introduced it is important to have your child say it correctly. Have your child practice saying the "short *i*" words on this page out loud several times.

■ Say the word represented by the picture out loud. Then circle the letter that makes the short "i" sound.

wig

hip

tin

dig

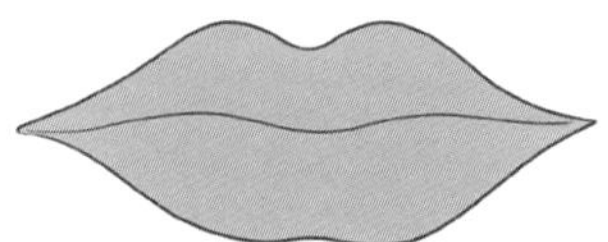

lips

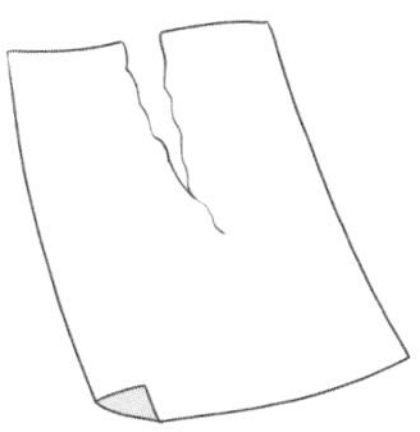

rip

sip

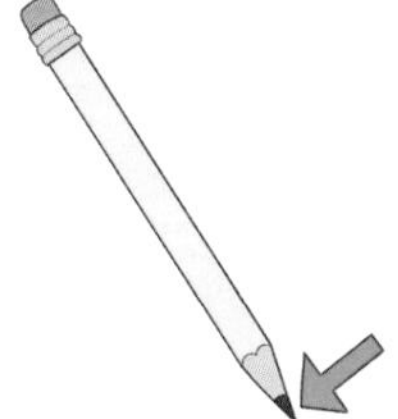

tip

a b c d e f g h i j k l m n o p q r s t u v w x y z

■ Draw a line along the path from the dot (●) to the star (★).
Each time you pass an image, say the word out loud.

a b c d e f g h i j k l m n o p q r s t u v w x y z

Vowel Sounds

Recognizing the Short "i" Sound

Name Date / /

To parents/guardians: If your child has trouble identifying the short vowel sound, have them practice saying the words out loud over and over. It is important to make sure your child knows each short vowel sound before moving on to the next.

■ Say the words represented by the pictures out loud. Two words in each row have the short "i" sound. Circle them.

sun  hip  pig

wig  dig 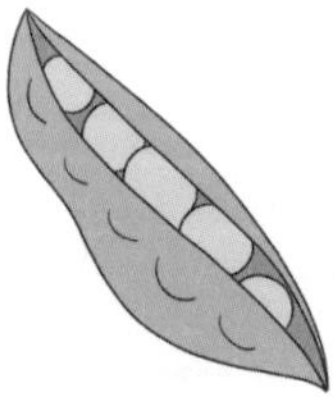 peas

key  tin 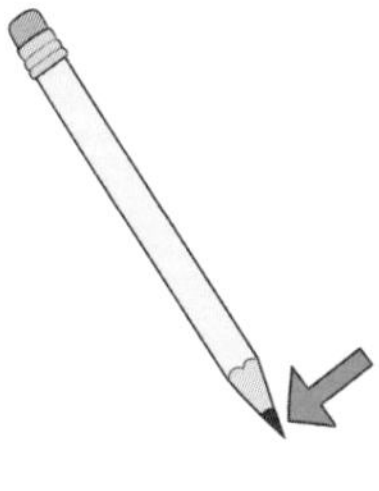 tip

a b c d e f g h i j k l m n o p q r s t u v w x y z

■ Say the words represented by the pictures out loud.
One word in each group has the short "i" sound. Circle it.

a b c d e f g h i j k l m n o p q r s t u v w x y z

Vowel Sounds

The Short "o" Sound

Name

Date

/ /

To parents/guardians: Long vowel sounds will be addressed in the next book of this series. It is important for your child to first become confident with short vowel sounds.

■ Say the word represented by the picture out loud.
Then circle the letter that makes the short "o" sound.

d o g

h o t

f o g

p o p

m o p

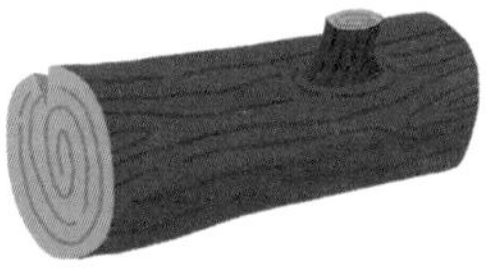

l o g

c o p

m o m

t o p

a b c d e f g h i j k l m n o p q r s t u v w x y z

■ Draw a line along the path from the dot (●) to the star (★).
Each time you pass an image, say the word out loud.

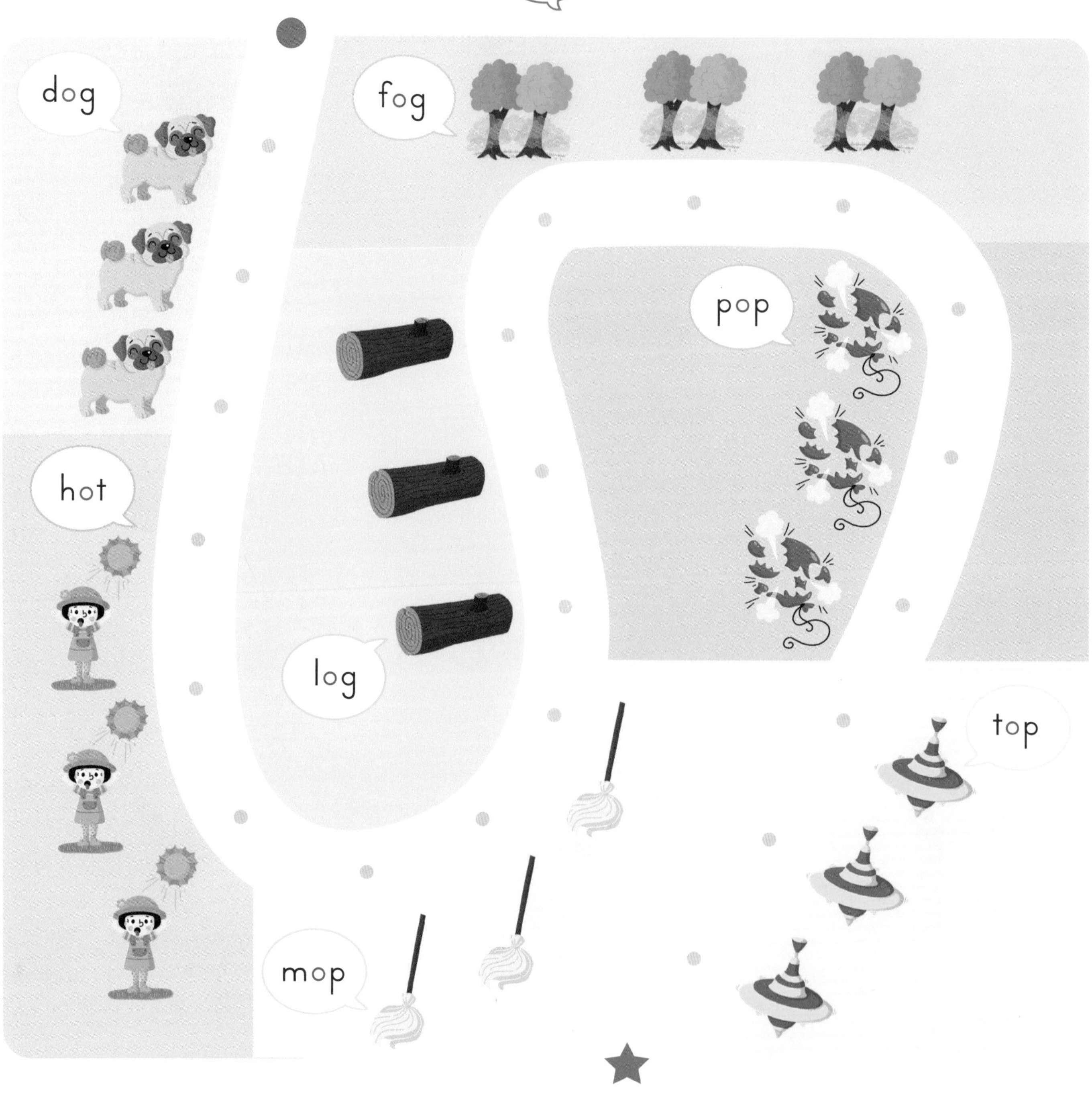

a b c d e f g h i j k l m n o p q r s t u v w x y z

Vowel Sounds

Recognizing the Short "o" Sound

Name Date / /

To parents/guardians: If your child struggles to say the "short *o*" words on this page, you can practice other "short *o*" words with them outside of this book. The more your child sees and says "short *o*" words, the easier they will recognize the sound the vowel makes.

■ Say the words represented by the pictures out loud.
Two words in each row have the short "o" sound. Circle them.

mop  day  fog

hot  dog  gap

top  tie  mom

a b c d e f g h i j k l m n o p q r s t u v w x y z

■ Say the words represented by the pictures out loud.
One word in each group has the short "o" sound. Circle it.

a b c d e f g h i j k l m n o p q r s t u v w x y z

42 Vowel Sounds

The Short "u" Sound

Name　　　　Date　　/　　/

To parents/guardians: Have your child think of other words with the short "u" sound. The more your child practices saying short "u" words, the better they will get at making the correct sound.

■ Say the word represented by the picture out loud. Then circle the letter that makes the short "u" sound.

s u n

m u g

h u g

r u n

g u m

n u t

c u t

c u p

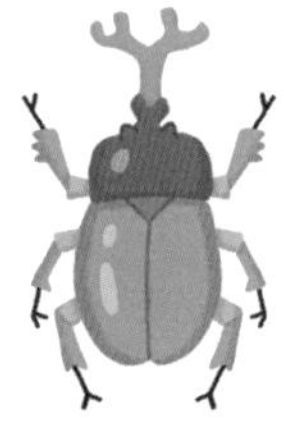

b u g

a b c d e f g h i j k l m n o p q r s t u v w x y z

■ Draw a line along the path from the dot (●) to the star (★). Each time you pass an image, say the word out loud.

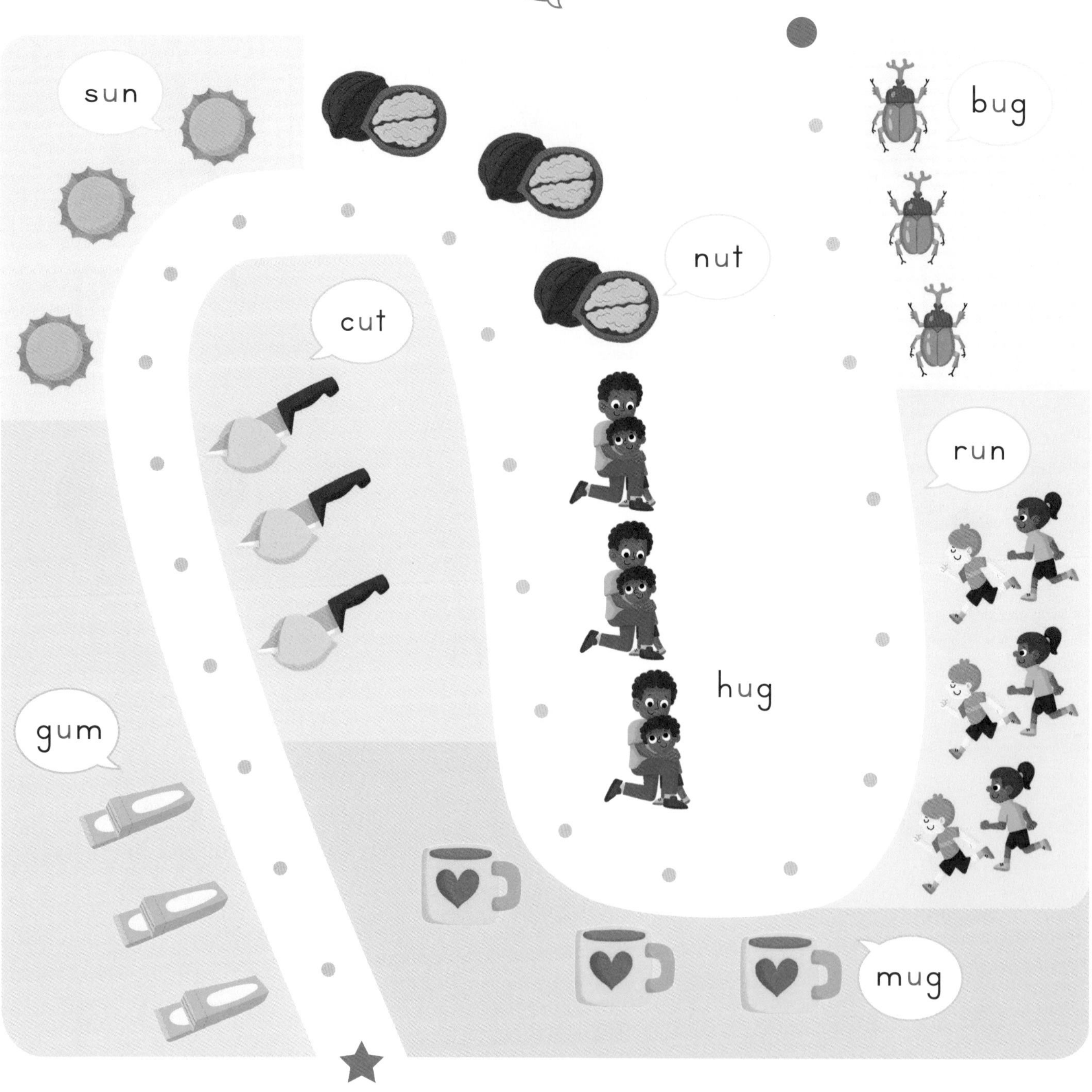

a b c d e f g h i j k l m n o p q r s t u v w x y z

Vowel Sounds

Recognizing the Short "u" Sound

Name

Date

/ /

To parents/guardians: If your child needs help with this activity, remind them to say the three words in each group. They should listen for the two words that rhyme.

■ Say the words represented by the pictures out loud.
Two words in each row have the short "u" sound. Circle them.

mug  hug  top

nut  fish  bug

hay  gum  cup

a b c d e f g h i j k l m n o p q r s t u v w x y z

■ Say the words represented by the pictures out loud.
One word in each group has the short "u" sound. Circle it.

a b c d e f g h i j k l m n o p q r s t u v w x y z

Vowel Review

The Short "a" and "e" Sounds

Name

Date / /

To parents/guardians: Here your child will review the short vowels in this section. Make sure they say each word out loud using the picture for help as they work through the page.

■ Say the word represented by the picture out loud. Then write in the missing letter.

m a p   b g   p n

w e t

p n

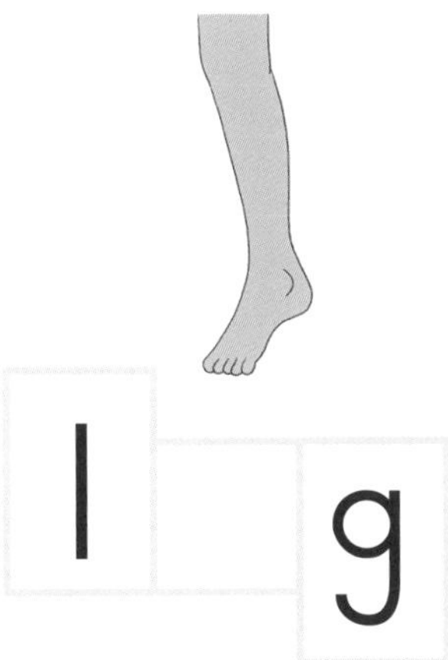

l g

a b c d e f g h i j k l m n o p q r s t u v w x y z

To parents/guardians: On this page, your child will find and say the words that still need coloring. They will then color in those words based on the vowel sound they hear in each. If your child has difficulty, go back to the short vowel pages and practice saying the words out loud again.

■ Color the pictures in this scene, using the key below. Say the words out loud as you go.

short a = red **short** e = blue

a b c d e f g h i j k l m n o p q r s t u v w x y z

Vowel Review

The Short "i", "o", and "u" Sounds

Name

Date

/ /

To parents/guardians: On this page, your child will review the short vowels learned in previous pages. Offer them help if they have trouble identifying the missing vowels. Your child can use the alphabet line along the bottom of this page for help.

■ Say the word represented by the picture out loud. Then write in the missing letter.

p i g

h p

k d

p o t

p p

l g

s u n

r n

n t

a b c d e f g h i j k l m n o p q r s t u v w x y z

To parents/guardians: This is the last page in this workbook. If your child has completed all the pages, offer them a lot of praise for their hard work! Then, give your child the "Certificate of Achievement" at the end of this book.

■ Color the pictures in this scene, using the key below. Say the words out loud as you go.

short i = red **short** o = orange **short** u = yellow

a b c d e f g h i j k l m n o p q r s t u v w x y z

My Book of Reading Skills: Easy Phonics Answer Key

1 Alphabet Review
Connect the Dots
Draw a line from a to z in alphabetical order while saying each letter out loud.

page 1

Draw a line from a to z in alphabetical order while saying each letter out loud.

page 2

2 Alphabet Review
Writing a–z
Trace the letters a to z.
a b c d
e f g h
i j k l
m n o p
q r s t
u v w x
y z

page 3

Write the letters a to z.
a b c d
e f g h
i j k l
m n o p
q r s t
u v w x
y z

page 4

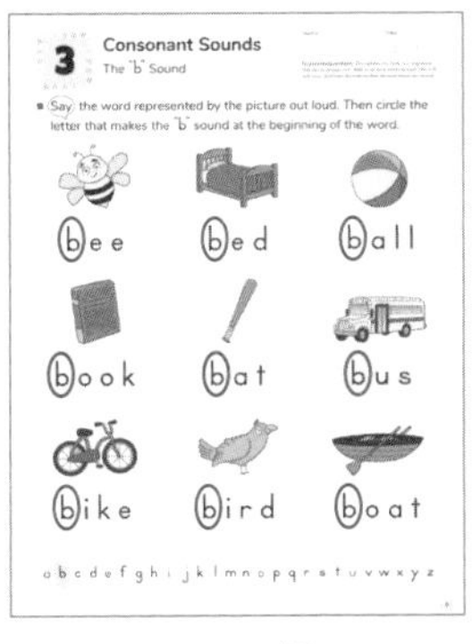
3 Consonant Sounds
The "b" Sound
Say the word represented by the picture out loud. Then circle the letter that makes the "b" sound at the beginning of the word.
bee bed ball
book bat bus
bike bird boat

page 5

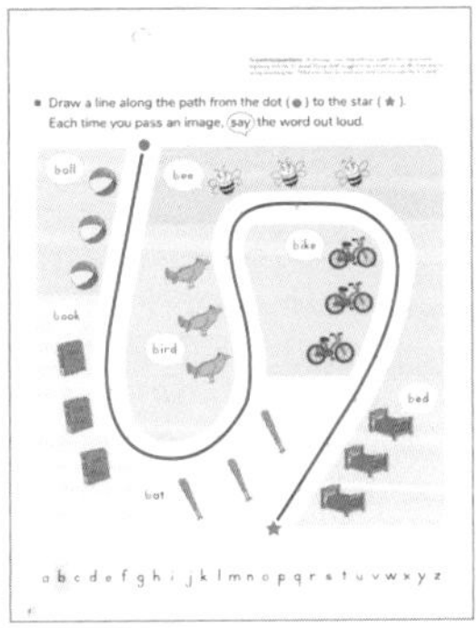
Draw a line along the path from the dot (●) to the star (★). Each time you pass an image, say the word out loud.

page 6

4 Consonant Sounds
The "k" Sound
Say the word represented by the picture out loud. Then circle the letter that makes the "k" sound at the beginning of the word.
key kid kite
kiss kick king
kitten kitchen koala

page 7

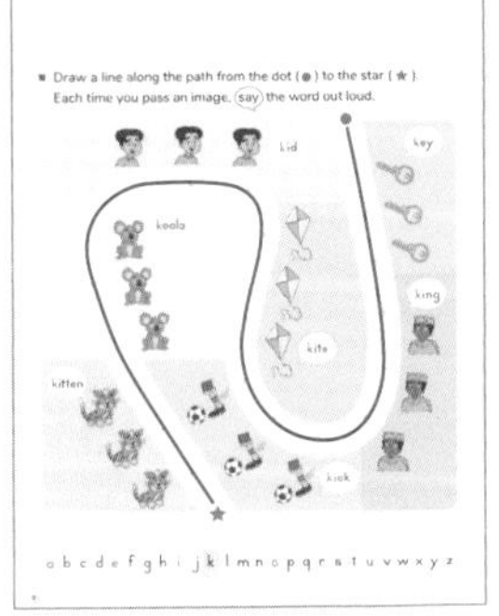
Draw a line along the path from the dot (●) to the star (★). Each time you pass an image, say the word out loud.

page 8

5 Consonant Sounds
The "p" Sound
Say the word represented by the picture out loud. Then circle the letter that makes the "p" sound at the beginning of the word.
pot pencil pink
penguin puddle peas
pond push plane

page 9

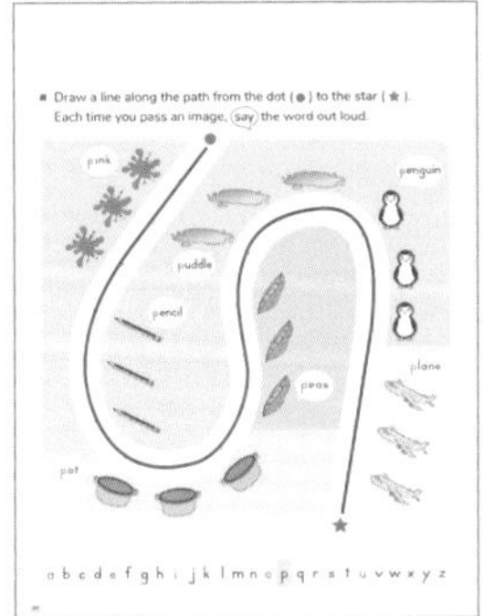
Draw a line along the path from the dot (●) to the star (★). Each time you pass an image, say the word out loud.

page 10

6 Consonant Review
The "b," "k," and "p" Sounds
Say the word represented by the picture out loud. Then write in the missing letter.
bee ball bike
key king kite
pot pink peas

page 11

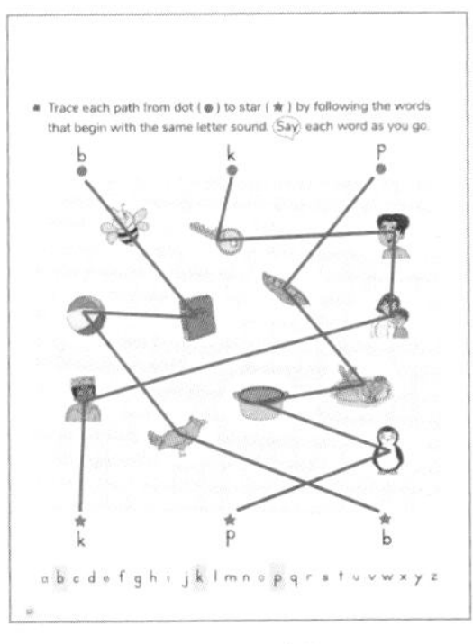
Trace each path from dot (●) to star (★) by following the words that begin with the same letter sound. Say each word as you go.

page 12

7 Consonant Sounds
The "t" Sound
Say the word represented by the picture out loud. Then circle the letter that makes the "t" sound at the beginning of the word.
tent top talk
tie tall table
tail tooth tiger

page 13

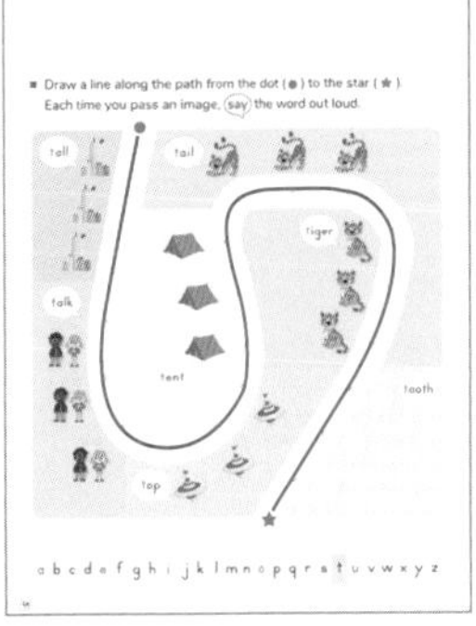
Draw a line along the path from the dot (●) to the star (★). Each time you pass an image, say the word out loud.

page 14

8 Consonant Sounds
The "d" Sound
Say the word represented by the picture out loud. Then circle the letter that makes the "d" sound at the beginning of the word.
duck desk deer
day doll donut
dress dry drum

page 15

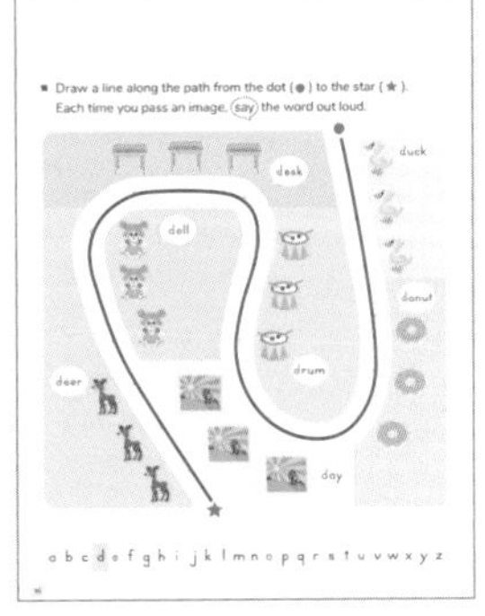
Draw a line along the path from the dot (●) to the star (★). Each time you pass an image, say the word out loud.

page 16

9 Consonant Sounds
The Hard "g" Sound
Say the word represented by the picture out loud. Then circle the letter that makes the hard "g" sound at the beginning of the word.
girl gold gift
goat go glue
gap grow green

page 17

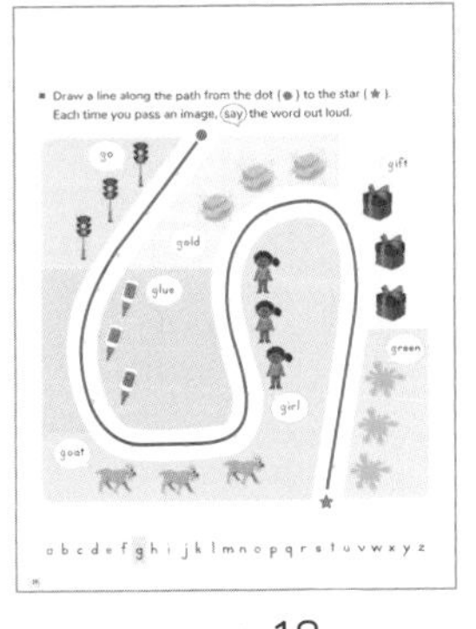
Draw a line along the path from the dot (●) to the star (★). Each time you pass an image, say the word out loud.

page 18

My Book of Reading Skills: Easy Phonics Answer Key

10 Consonant Review
The "t", "d", and Hard "g" Sounds
Say the word represented by the picture out loud. Then write in the missing letter.
tie tent tiger
duck drum doll
go gift green

page 19

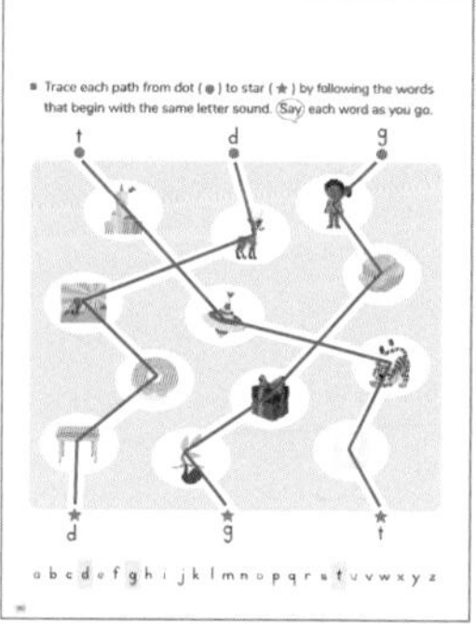
Trace each path from dot (●) to star (★) by following the words that begin with the same letter sound. Say each word as you go.

page 20

11 Consonant Sounds
The Hard "c" Sound
Say the word represented by the picture out loud. Then circle the letter that makes the hard "c" sound at the beginning of the word.
car call coat
card carrot crab
cold cake corn

page 21

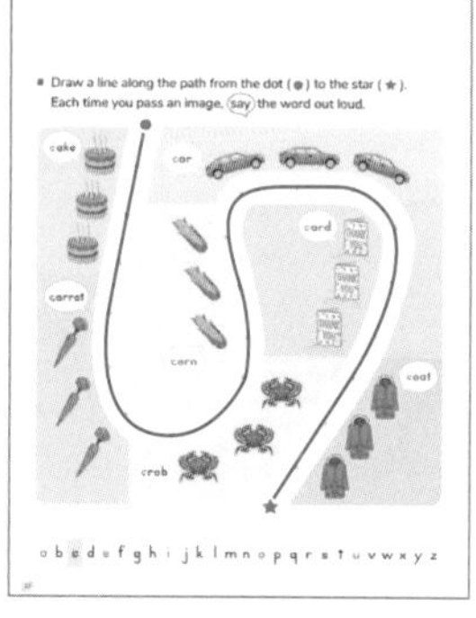
Draw a line along the path from the dot (●) to the star (★). Each time you pass an image, say the word out loud.

page 22

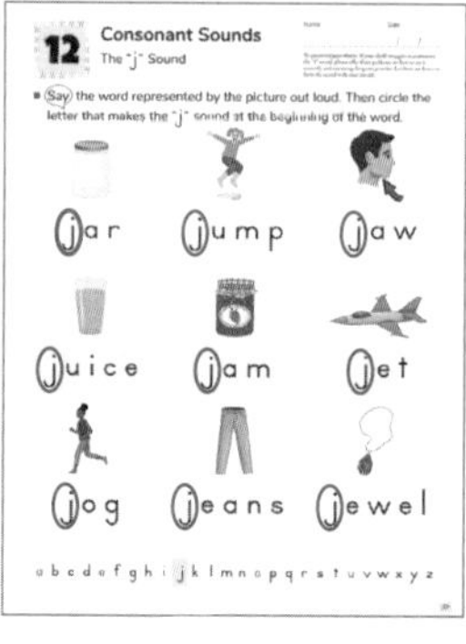
12 Consonant Sounds
The "j" Sound
Say the word represented by the picture out loud. Then circle the letter that makes the "j" sound at the beginning of the word.
jar jump jaw
juice jam jet
jog jeans jewel

page 23

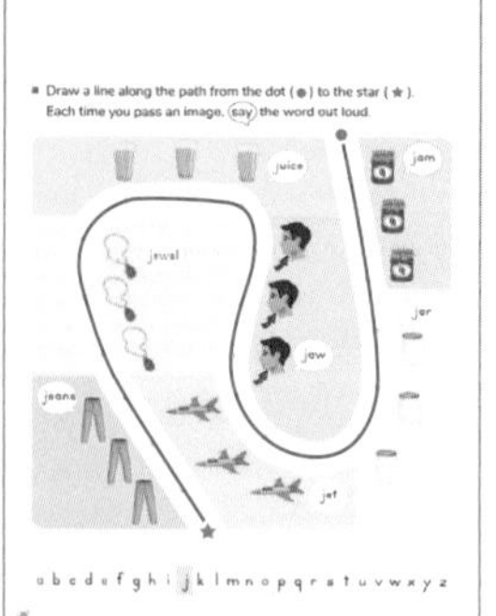
Draw a line along the path from the dot (●) to the star (★). Each time you pass an image, say the word out loud.

page 24

13 Consonant Sounds
The "m" Sound
Say the word represented by the picture out loud. Then circle the letter that makes the "m" sound at the beginning of the word.
mail mouse man
mask muffin milk
moon mouth money

page 25

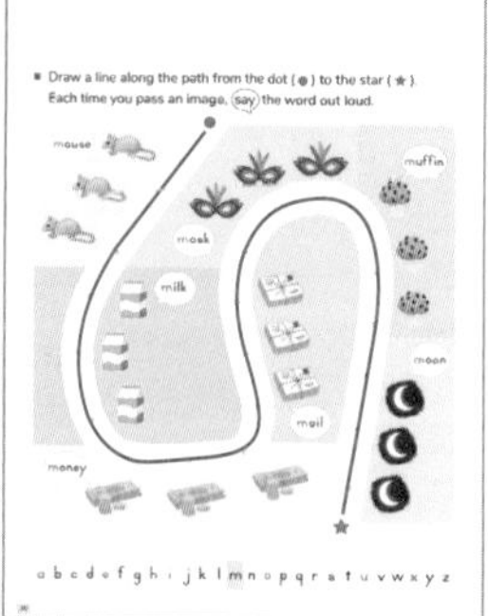
Draw a line along the path from the dot (●) to the star (★). Each time you pass an image, say the word out loud.

page 26

14 Consonant Review
The Hard "c", "j", and "m" Sounds
Say the word represented by the picture out loud. Then write in the missing letter.
car cake corn
jar jam jewel
mail milk moon

page 27

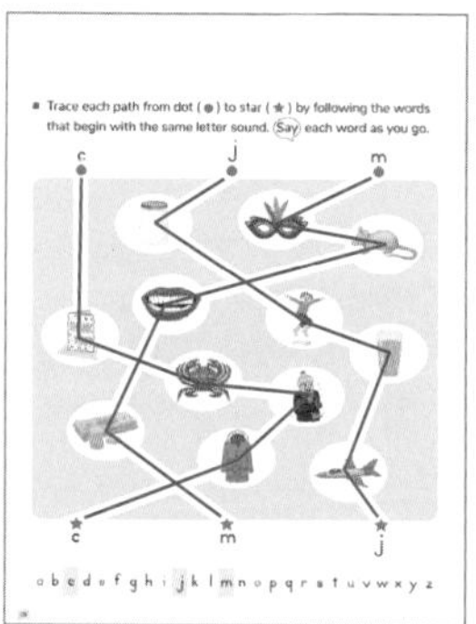
Trace each path from dot (●) to star (★) by following the words that begin with the same letter sound. Say each word as you go.

page 28

15 Consonant Sounds
The "s" Sound
Say the word represented by the picture out loud. Then circle the letter that makes the "s" sound at the beginning of the word.
six sand sip
salt sock snake
sing spin soap

page 29

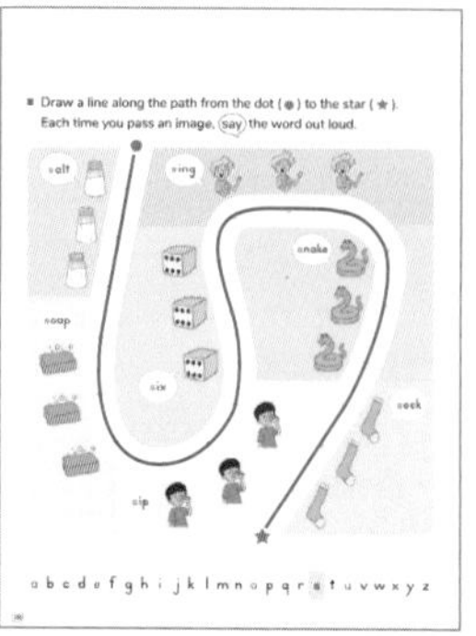
Draw a line along the path from the dot (●) to the star (★). Each time you pass an image, say the word out loud.

page 30

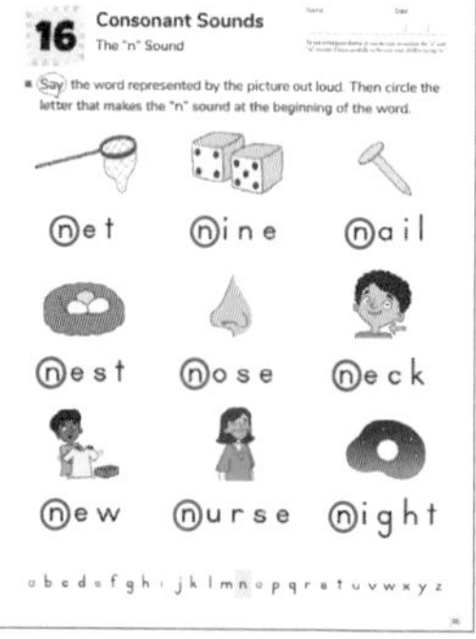
16 Consonant Sounds
The "n" Sound
Say the word represented by the picture out loud. Then circle the letter that makes the "n" sound at the beginning of the word.
net nine nail
nest nose neck
new nurse night

page 31

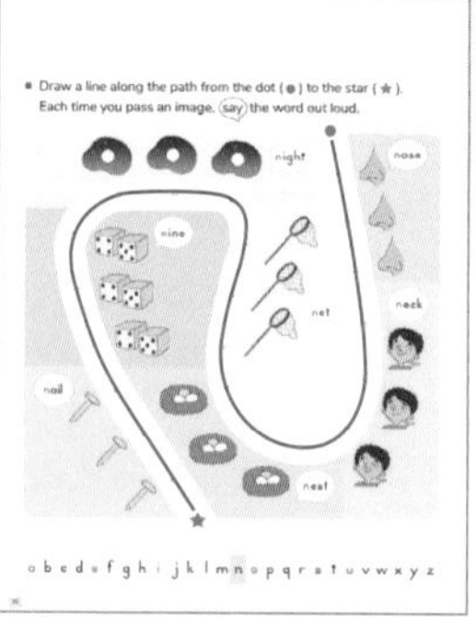
Draw a line along the path from the dot (●) to the star (★). Each time you pass an image, say the word out loud.

page 32

17 Consonant Sounds
The "l" Sound
Say the word represented by the picture out loud. Then circle the letter that makes the "l" sound at the beginning of the word.
lion leg lid
lips last lamp
lock lake lawn

page 33

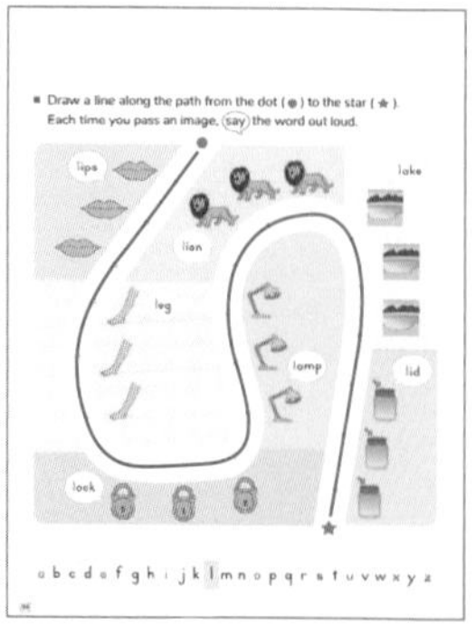
Draw a line along the path from the dot (●) to the star (★). Each time you pass an image, say the word out loud.

page 34

18 Consonant Review
The "s", "n", and "l" Sounds
Say the word represented by the picture out loud. Then write in the missing letter.
sip salt six
net new nest
lips leg lid

page 35

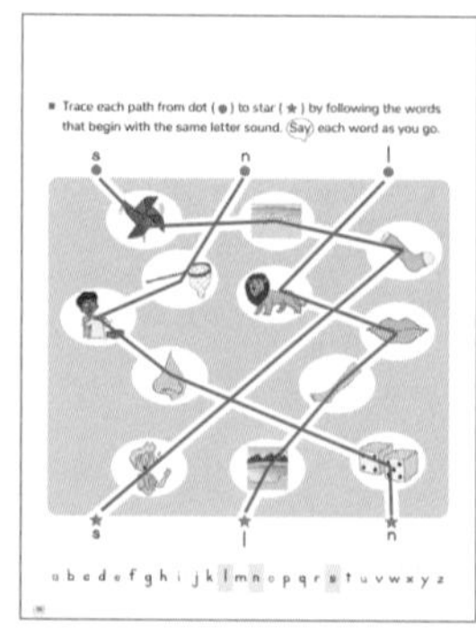
Trace each path from dot (●) to star (★) by following the words that begin with the same letter sound. Say each word as you go.

page 36

My Book of Reading Skills: Easy Phonics Answer Key

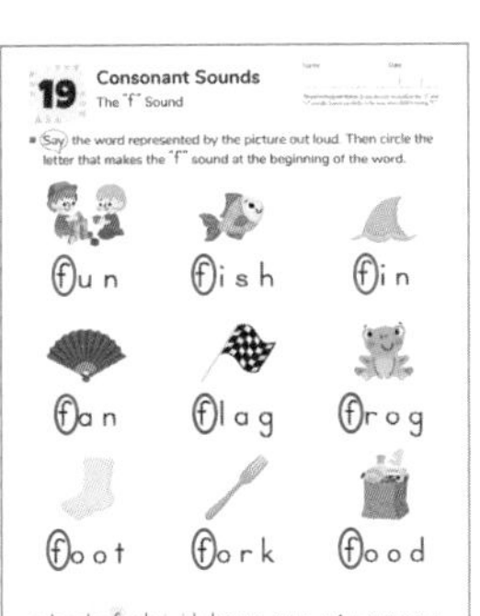
page 37

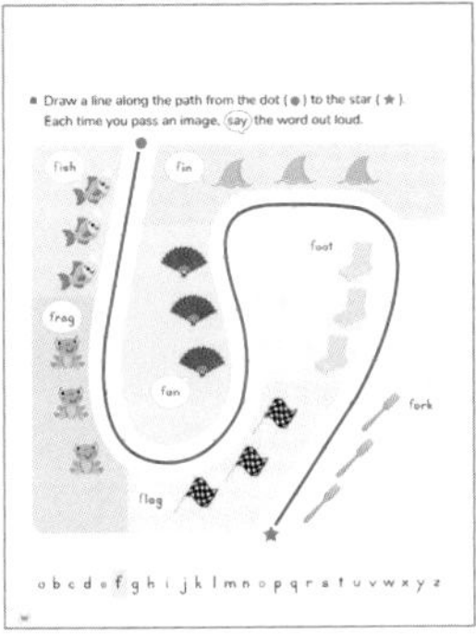
page 38

page 39

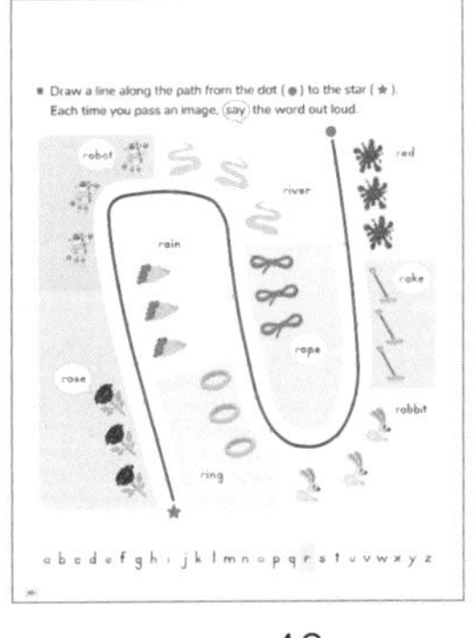
page 40

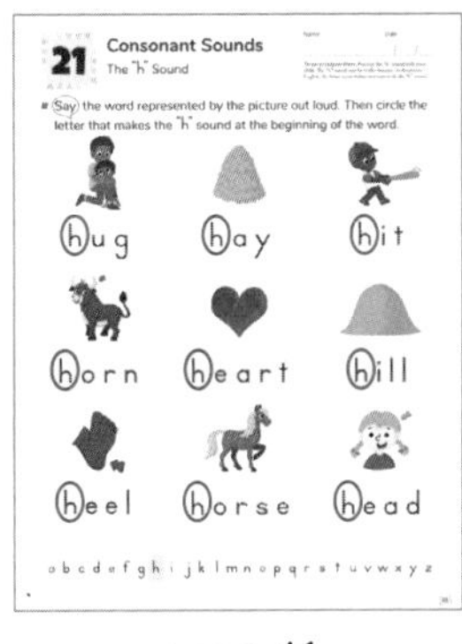
page 41

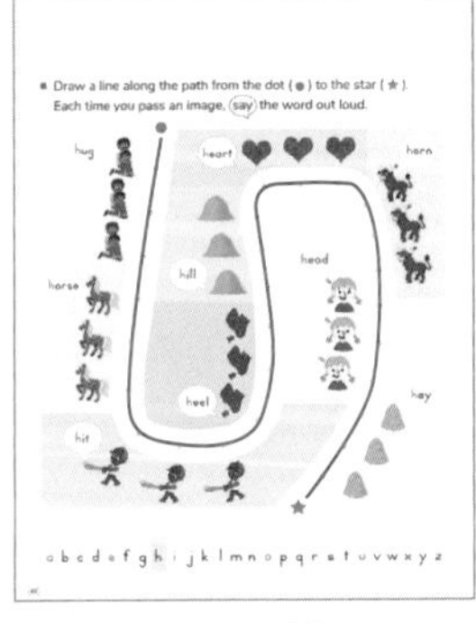
page 42

page 43

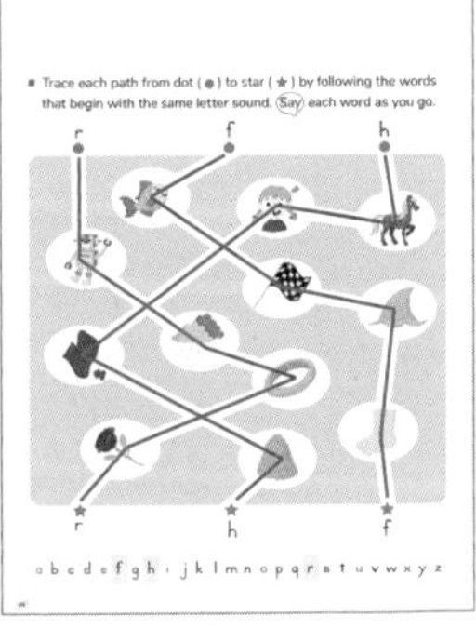
page 44

page 45

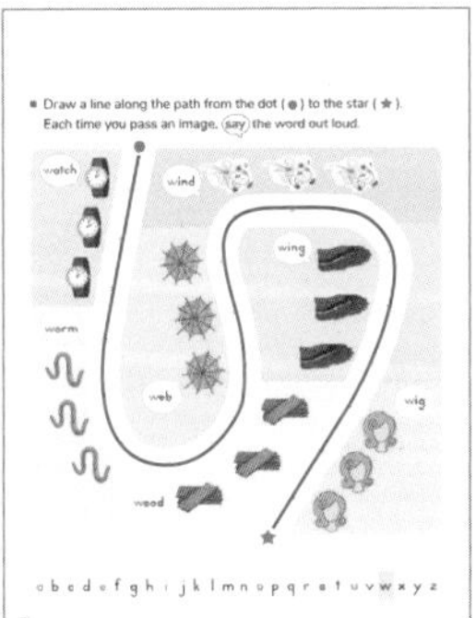
page 46

page 47

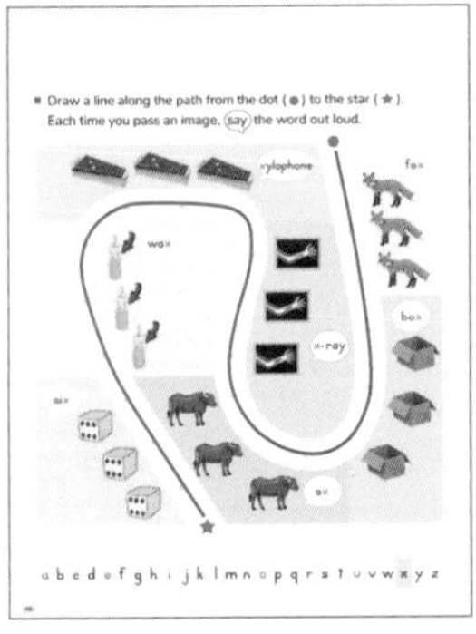
page 48

page 49

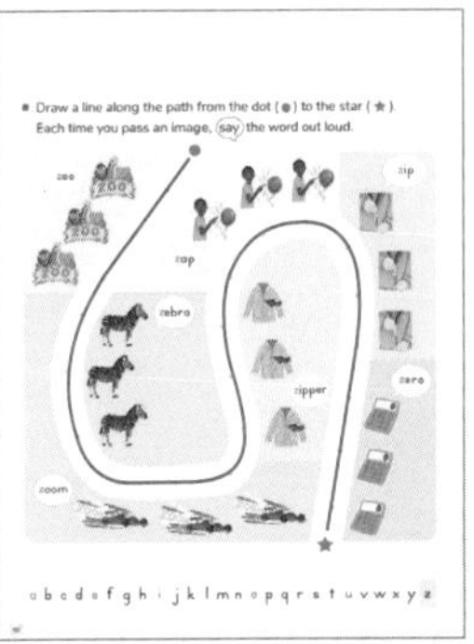
page 50

page 51

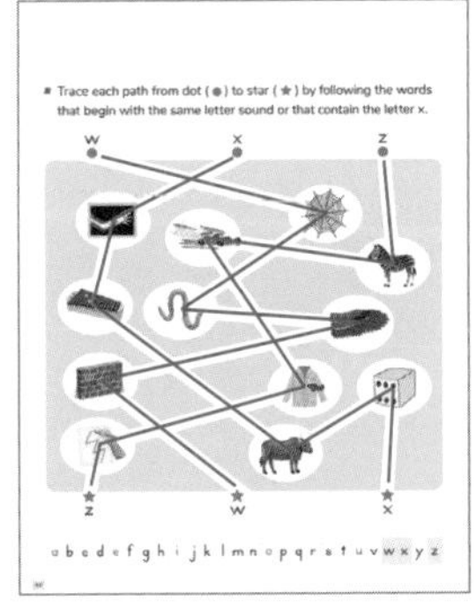
page 52

page 53

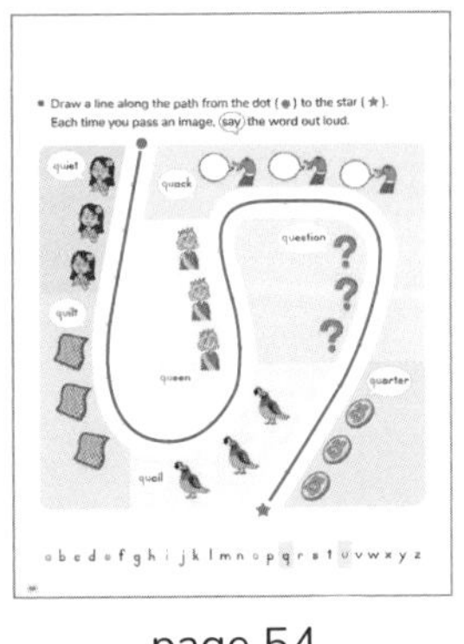
page 54

My Book of Reading Skills: Easy Phonics Answer Key

page 55

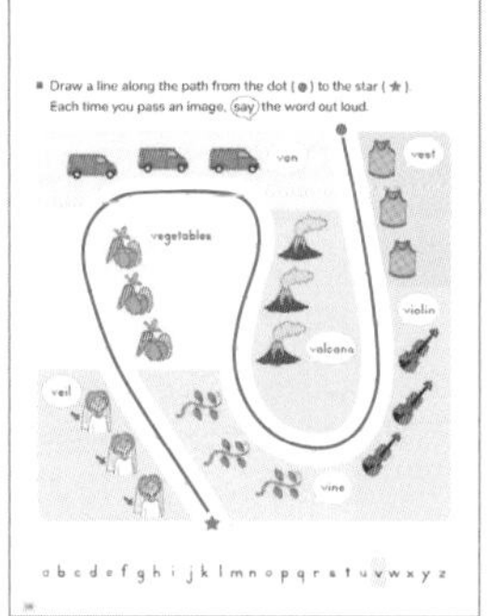
page 56

page 57

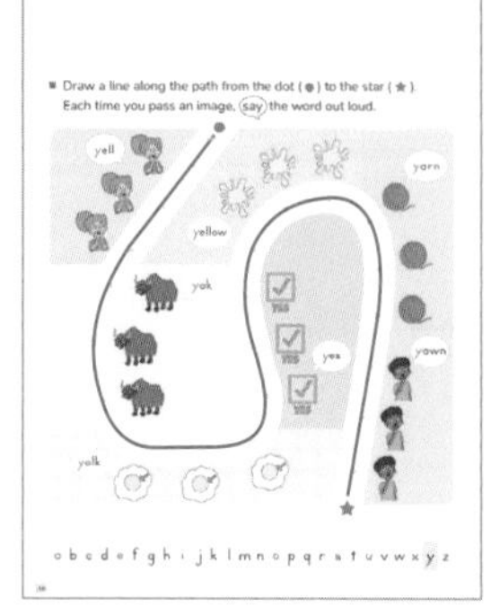
page 58

page 59

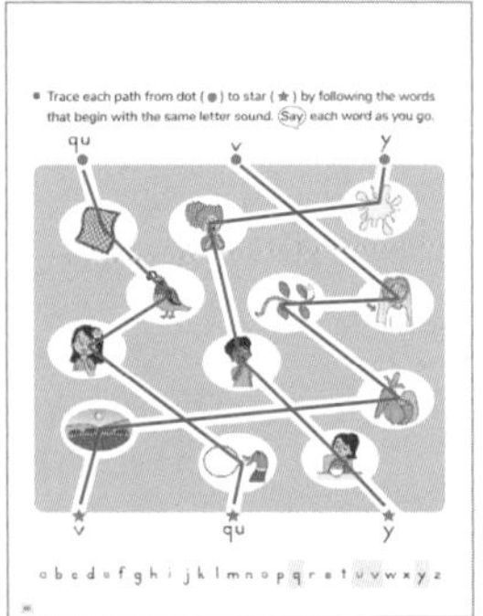
page 60

page 61

page 62

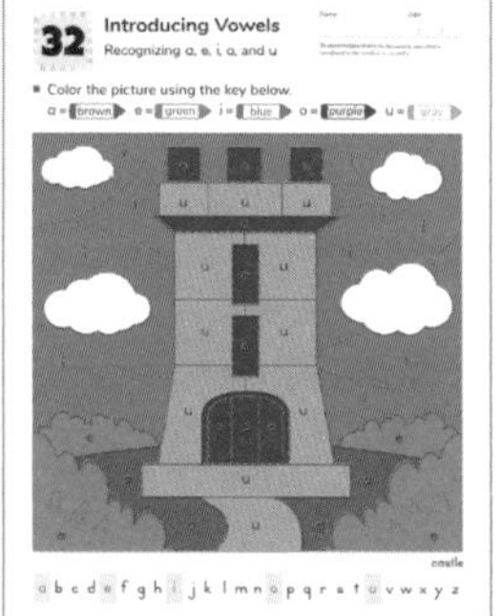
page 63

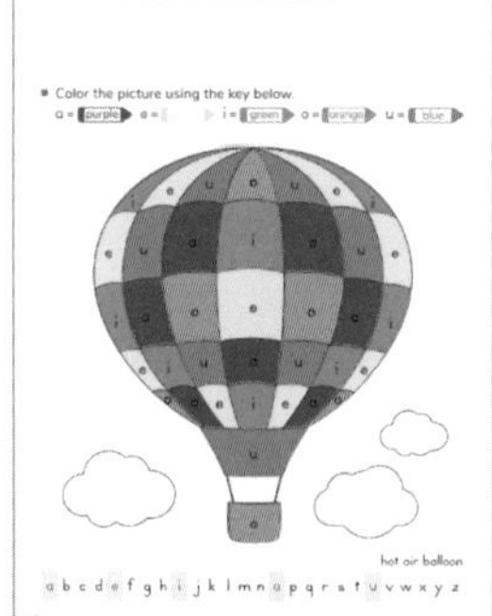
page 64

page 65

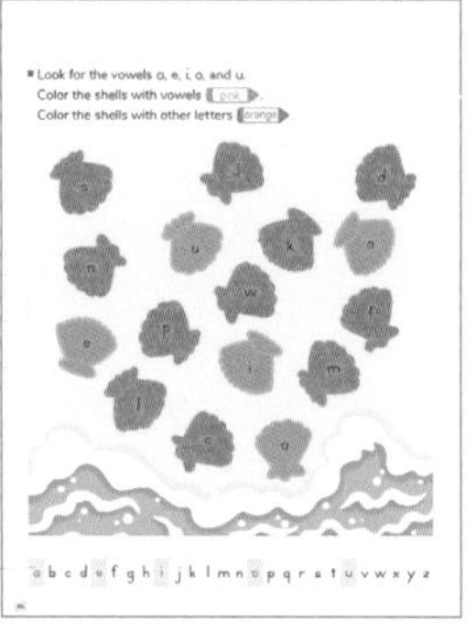
page 66

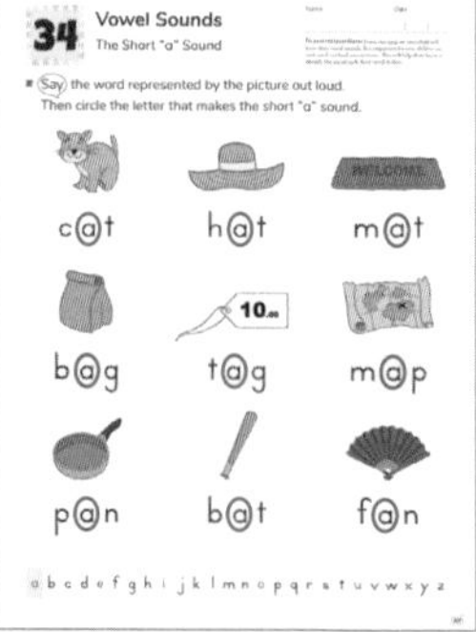
page 67

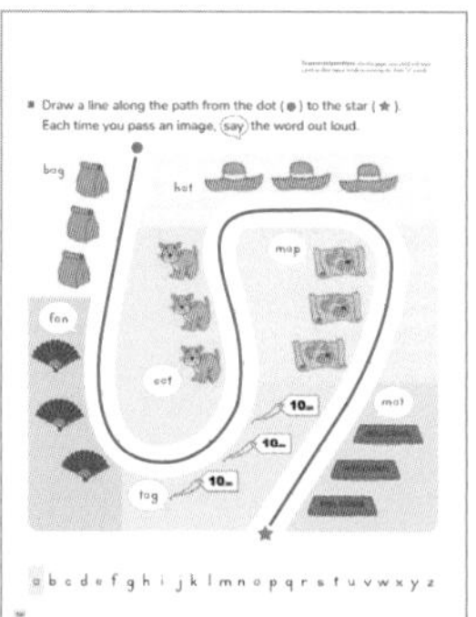
page 68

page 69

page 70

page 71

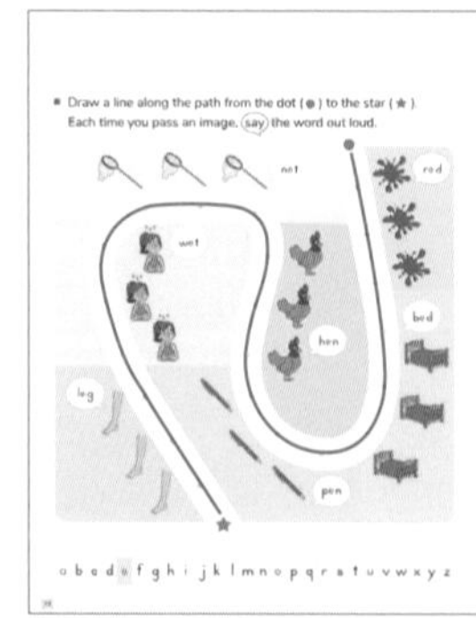
page 72

My Book of Reading Skills: Easy Phonics Answer Key

page 73

page 74

page 75

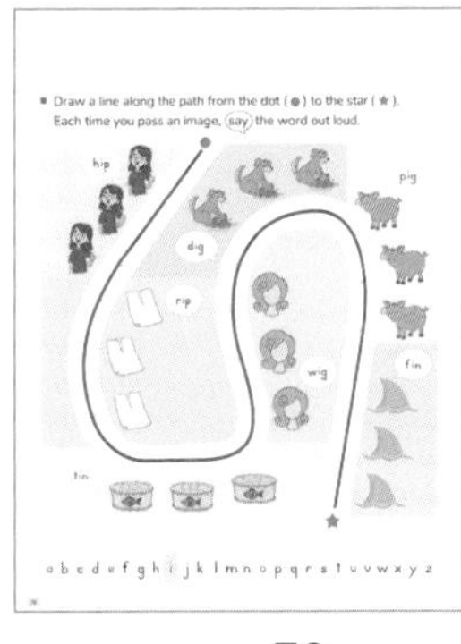
page 76

page 77

page 78

page 79

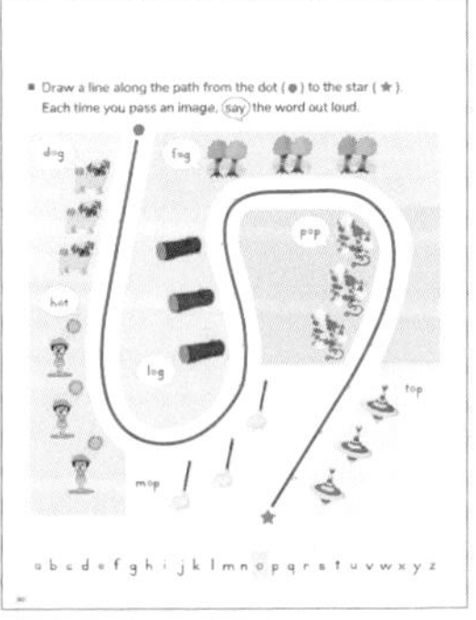
page 80

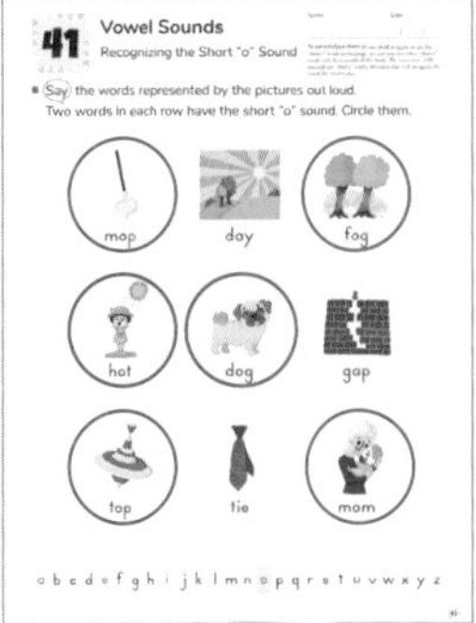
page 81

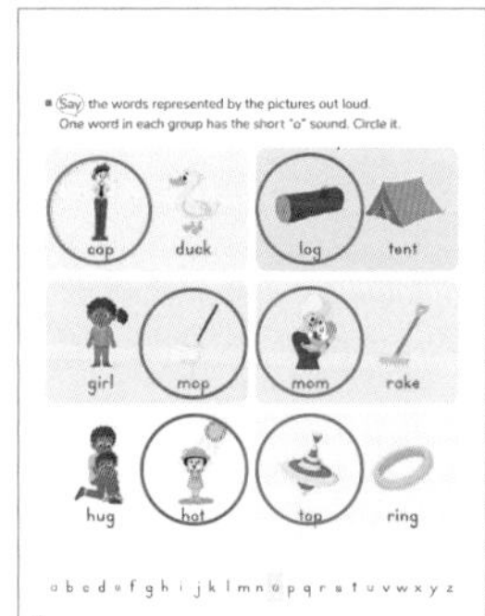
page 82

page 83

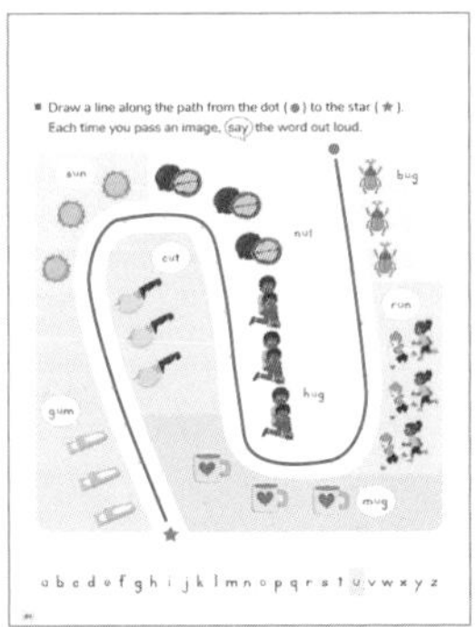
page 84

page 85

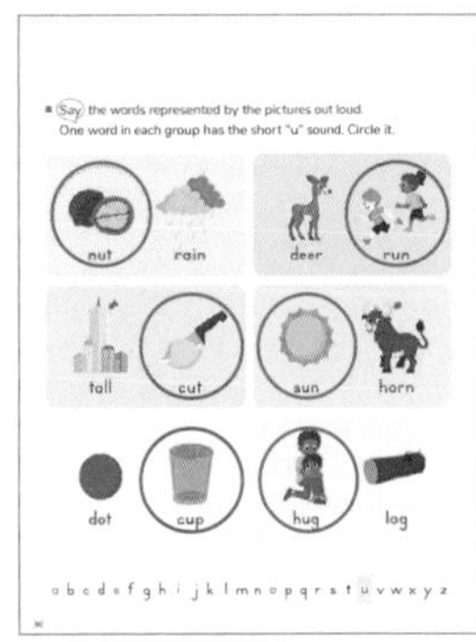
page 86

page 87

page 88

page 89

page 90

Certificate of Achievement

is hereby congratulated on completing

My Book of Reading Skills: Easy Phonics

Presented on , 20

Parent or guardian